VEGAN FOR ONE

hot tips AND inspired recipes FOR cooking solo

Ellen Jaffe Jones
Beverly Lynn Bennett

Book Publishing Company
SUMMERTOWN, TENNESSEE

Library of Congress Cataloging-in-Publication Data

Names: Jones, Ellen Jaffe, author. | Bennett, Beverly Lynn, author.
Title: Vegan for one : hot tips and inspired recipes for cooking solo / Ellen
    Jaffe Jones, Beverly Lynn Bennett.
Description: Summertown, Tennessee : Book Publishing Company, [2017] |
    Includes index.
Identifiers: LCCN 2017021873 (print) | LCCN 2017026429 (ebook) | ISBN
    9781570678509 (E-book) | ISBN 9781570673511 (pbk.)
Subjects: LCSH: Vegan cooking. | LCGFT: Cookbooks.
Classification: LCC TX837 (ebook) | LCC TX837 .J54295 2017 (print) | DDC
    641.5/636—dc23
LC record available at https://lccn.loc.gov/2017021873

Nutrition Breakdowns for Recipes: The nutrient values provided for the recipes in this book are estimates only, calculated from the individual ingredients used in each recipe based on the nutrition data found for those ingredients. Optional items are not included. Nutrient content may vary based on methods of preparation, origin and freshness of ingredients, product brands, and other factors.

We chose to print this title on responsibly harvested paper stock certified by The Forest Stewardship Council, an independent auditor of responsible forestry practices. For more information, visit us.fsc.org.

Cover and interior design: John Wincek
Food styling and photography: Alan Roettinger
Stock photography: 123 RF

Printed in Canada

Book Publishing Company
PO Box 99
Summertown, TN 38483
888-260-8458
bookpubco.com

ISBN: 978-1-57067-351-1

22 21 20 19 18 17   1 2 3 4 5 6 7 8 9

Disclaimer: The information in this book is presented for educational purposes only. It isn't intended to be a substitute for the medical advice of a physician, dietitian, or other healthcare professional.

CONTENTS

ACKNOWLEDGMENTS

I consider my parents to be my own personal rock stars. My dad gave me an appreciation for natural foods with his organic garden, and my mom was an eloquent writer. Thanks to the fact they had me late in life, I got some early experience in solo living as an almost-only child!

My deep appreciation to Steve Cantor for helping me understand that a life as a TV network correspondent was not as important as having a life. He left this world way too soon.

Thanks to my three daughters, Rebecca, Jessica, and Aron, who continue to motivate me every day to have a life of purpose and make the world a better place. They accompanied me on my first solo forays into vegan eating (well, they were too young to have much of a choice!), and I appreciate how they shared the adventure with me.

Kudos to Bob and Cynthia Holzapfel at Book Publishing Company, who had the vision for this book's concept and asked if it rang true for me. Indeed it has for much of my life.

My gratitude to senior editor Jo Stepaniak for sewing together the frayed loose ends of this text and making the words jump off the page. Many thanks to Anna Pope, John Schweri, Alayne Griffin, Dave Weaverling, and Michael Thomas, who work tirelessly behind the scenes making books and events happen like magic.

Much appreciation to Beverly Lynn Bennett, whose culinary wizardry demonstrates how small-quantity recipes can have all the flavor and pizazz one could want.

Thanks to Val McDaniel, who has challenged me to new heights in writing and cooking and promoting a vegan lifestyle that is so good for our health, the planet, and the animals.

Alone is how we enter and leave the world, and sometimes how we live a significant portion of it in between. Aloneness, not to be confused with loneliness, is necessary for self-love, wisdom, and inner peace. On our own, we discover who we really are and what motivates us. No matter how you travel through life, as a vegan you will always have the gratitude of the earth and the animals. May these recipes sustain and help you thrive along that journey.

Ellen Jaffe Jones

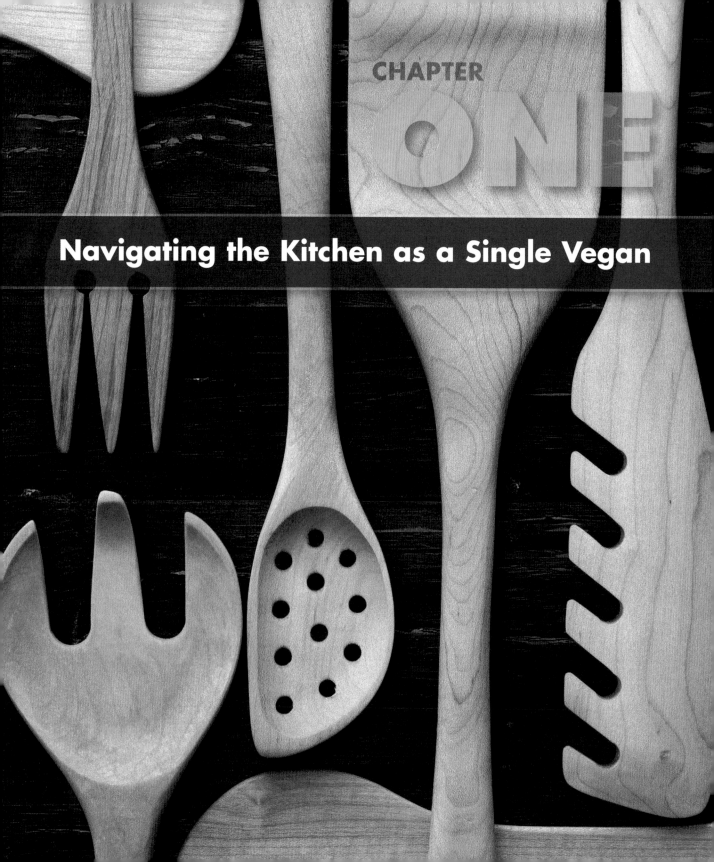

Navigating the Kitchen as a Single Vegan

YOU'RE IN GOOD COMPANY!

Solo living, whether by choice or circumstance, has never been more appealing, satisfying, and fulfilling as it is today. Living alone used to be the stigma and dread of old age, but now it's often a sign of independence. You can come and go as you choose, you don't have to be accountable to anyone for your time or choices, and at the end of a long day, the solitude of your own home or apartment can be comforting and relaxing. Most major cities have revitalized downtown areas where singles can find accommodations and amenities that facilitate socializing.

As a single vegan, you're in good company. The US Census found in 2015 that 109 million people age eighteen and older were single. This is equivalent to 34 percent of all US residents. A poll conducted early in the decade by the Vegetarian Resource Group showed that 2–3 percent of the US population is vegan. With the population topping 320 million today, that would mean six to ten million people in the United States are vegan and two to three million of those vegans are living by themselves. The popularity of vegetarianism in general is evident even on a global scale. Estimates for the number of vegetarians in Germany range from 8–9 percent of the population, and for Israel 5–6 percent. India boasts the first all-vegetarian city, Palitana, in the state of Gujarat, just north of Mumbai.

What accounts for the growing numbers of vegans? For starters, studies show that vegans live longer, maintain healthier weights, and suffer from fewer diseases than their meat-eating counterparts. But athletes are also turning to vegan diets to improve recovery rates, reduce the incidence of injury, and increase their energy, endurance, and performance.

In addition, people of all ages are increasingly concerned about the ethical and environmental consequences of eating animal products. The United Nations Food and Agriculture Organization released its landmark findings in 2006 on the relationship between food animals and environmental degradation in its report "Livestock's Long Shadow." I personally came face-to-face with the inhumanity of animal mistreatment when I was a TV reporter in Miami. The more I investigated, the more I realized that this abuse is a routine aspect of the food-animal industry, not just a misfortune that befalls shelter animals.

SUCCESSFUL MEAL STRATEGIES FOR THE SINGLE VEGAN

If you're newly vegan, you might not know exactly what to eat to sustain your energy and stay healthy. There are a number of excellent sources for reliable information, such as *Becoming Vegan: Express Edition* (by veteran vegans and registered dietitians Brenda Davis and Vesanto Melina) and the Vegetarian Resource Group (vrg.org). If you have special dietary needs—particularly if you're over sixty-five, an athlete, pregnant or nursing, or trying to lose or gain weight—these resources will help you address those needs. In general, center your diet around a variety of vegetables, fruits, beans, whole grains, and nuts and seeds. The Physicians Committee for Responsible Medicine (pcrm.org) offers the following daily recommendation: one cup or more of plant protein, three or more servings of fruits, four or more servings of vegetables, and five servings of whole grains. I'd add to that one tablespoon of whole-food fat via plant foods that are naturally high in fat, such as nuts, seeds, olives, or avocados—not oils derived from these foods. Nut butters without added sugar or salt would also do. As long as you follow this broad guideline—and supplement with vitamin B_{12}, the one nutrient you can't obtain through food on a vegan diet (and one that even meat eaters are often deficient in)—you should be getting everything you need. Purchase organic foods to ensure you're eating nutritious, high-quality foods that are free of chemical residues.

If this is the first time you're having to prep your own meals, you may not know where to begin. Take a tip from institutional menu planners: they know that most people are completely satisfied rotating among ten to twelve of their favorite meals, which offers plenty of variety with minimal repetition. Make a list of a dozen of your favorite dinners. If you're a planner, the list will help you shop for the ingredients you'll need. If you're the indecisive type, let your list make the choice for you and prepare whatever's next up in the rotation. If you'd rather follow your whims, keep the list on hand to provide inspiration or a starting point.

If you don't like cooking every night or you've been used to making enough food for a family, try teaming up with a friend or two and cook for each other. Making a meal together or taking turns at cooking is not only a lot less expensive than buying takeout, but it's also a fun opportunity for socializing. If friends and family haven't been interested in joining you on your vegan journey, check out information online or at local natural food stores about vegan groups in your area. There may be a number of local gatherings where you can meet like-minded people who might enjoy sharing meals.

One advantage of cooking just for yourself is that you can eat whatever you want, whenever you want it. You're not limited by someone else's preferences and requirements. You can rethink what a meal is—for instance, you can have breakfast for dinner or dinner for breakfast, if that's what you're up for. If pancakes and veggie sausage are calling to you at six p.m. or only bean burritos will do at dawn, no one else will care. Turn a typically sweet dish into something savory; for example, top waffles with scrambled tofu, chopped tomatoes, and grated vegan cheese. Instead of a cup of vegan yogurt with a little jam on the bottom, pour that yogurt over a big bowl of your favorite berries or sliced fruit and top it with chopped nuts for a hearty breakfast or dessert. Add nut butter and chopped spinach to a fruit smoothie for a full meal on the go.

If you're a senior solo vegan, be aware that your senses of smell and taste may diminish with age. As a result, you may shun variety in favor of a few select foods or meals that are intensely flavored. Be sure to include an assortment of brightly colored fruits and vegetables in your meals, and consider regular consultations with a health professional who's knowledgeable about vegan diets to ensure you're making wise choices and obtaining adequate nutrition.

LOOK FOR FOODS THAT KEEP WELL

One of the biggest challenges for a single vegan is eating foods before they spoil. When you're shopping, think about which foods will need to be eaten within a few days and which ones can be stored for a while. The following fruits and vegetables generally stay fresh longer than most other produce:

- Apples
- Beets
- Bell peppers
- Cabbages
- Carrots
- Garlic
- Kale
- Onions
- Pears
- Sweet potatoes
- White potatoes
- Winter squashes

Note that onions and white potatoes are best stored in a cool, dry place—not in the refrigerator. Keep in mind that whole, uncut produce will keep longer than fruits and vegetables that have been cut and packaged. Prepared produce can be a great time-saver, but it can be a lot more costly, especially if you don't end up using it before it goes bad. Consider buying just a few apples or potatoes or one onion at a time instead of a whole bag. And check out your store's salad bar; there's usually an array of assorted fruits and veggies, so you can purchase small amounts of only what you need for a very reasonable price, and the prep is already done for you. While it's tempting to stock up, you can stretch your shopping dollars over a wider variety of foods by purchasing smaller quantities.

Make a note to eat the produce that won't keep long first. Use perishable leafy greens and sprouts in salads or sandwiches. Then keep an eye on slightly hardier foods, such as avocados, bananas, green onions, mushrooms, peaches, and tomatoes. If you have a vegetable that looks like it's past its prime, add it to a soup or stir-fry. Dip peaches or mangoes in boiling water for one minute, slip off their skins, remove the pits, and slice them; you can freeze them in single-serving portions in airtight storage containers. Peel bananas that have gotten too brown and freeze them whole in airtight storage containers; there's no need to wrap them individually. Frozen fruit is great to use in smoothies, as it will make them thick and creamy and impart richness without added fat.

If your produce routinely goes bad before you get to it, consider replacing the more delicate items you use in salads and sandwiches with hardier ones. For example, instead of bibb or looseleaf lettuce in your sandwiches, use romaine, Swiss chard, or kale. Make salads with sturdier greens, such as chopped mature kale or collards or baby kale instead of spinach or lettuce. Create chopped salads with layers of finely cut cabbage and kale, shredded carrots, and diced broccoli, beets, and celery, along with bean sprouts and chopped olives. Top them with the more delicate produce you need to use up—avocados, tender greens, tomatoes—and toss them with a hearty dressing that contains vegan mayo or nut butter as a base.

Although small containers of food cost more per ounce than larger containers, you won't save anything if the contents spoil before you can use them. Plant-based milks are especially perishable, so buy them in small containers so you can consume them before they become a science experiment.

STORE PRODUCE PROPERLY

Storing produce correctly once you get it home will help increase its shelf life. The produce drawers in many refrigerators have settings to adjust the humidity. Some produce holds up well in moist environments, but most will keep longer if the humidity is low. How can you tell which items do best in which environment? Look at the produce displays in your supermarket; notice which foods are regularly sprayed with water and which ones are kept dry in the center, and then follow their lead.

The following table lists common high-humidity and low-humidity fruits and vegetables.

HIGH-HUMIDITY PRODUCE	LOW-HUMIDITY PRODUCE
Beets	Apples
Broccoli	Bananas
Brussels sprouts	Blueberries
Cabbage	Garlic
Carrots	Grapefruits
Celery	Grapes
Green onions	Melons
Greens	Onions
Lettuce	Oranges
Mushrooms	Pears
Parsnips	Pineapples
Rutabagas	Potatoes, sweet
Spinach	Potatoes, white
Turnips	Strawberries

It's fun to cook with fresh herbs, such as basil and parsley, but how many little packages of them wilt beyond rescue before they're used up? Next time, put that bunch of herbs in a small glass of water, just as you would a bouquet of flowers, and cover it with waxed paper. You'll increase the amount of time the herbs stay fresh, and you'll be able to easily boost the flavor and nutrition of your meals simply by breaking off just the amount of the herb you want to add to a dish.

Some produce holds up best at room temperature, outside the refrigerator, particularly avocados (until they're soft), bananas, melons, onions, and potatoes. However, you can extend the life of an avocado that's just a bit soft at the stem end by storing it tightly wrapped in waxed paper in the low-humidity section of the refrigerator.

No produce items will keep well if the inside of your refrigerator is too warm. Invest in an inexpensive refrigerator thermometer, and keep the temperature between 35 and 38 degrees F. Organisms that cause foodborne illness markedly increase at temperatures above 40 degrees F. Don't pack your refrigerator tightly; space is needed between food items for air to circulate and maintain a constant temperature.

Finally, keep the inside of your refrigerator clean, especially those pesky produce drawers. If something spoils, bacteria and mold will be present on the inner walls of the fridge. It's a chore to empty out an entire refrigerator to clean it, so make a habit of wiping down shelves and rinsing out drawers with a non-abrasive cleanser right before you go grocery shopping, when the fridge is nearly empty. Also, keep cooked foods covered to protect them from contamination.

BEYOND FRESH PRODUCE: CANNED AND FROZEN TO THE RESCUE

The recipes in this book generally call for fresh fruits and vegetables, but let's face it, life happens. And for some reason it seems to happen most often right before dinner. When the unexpected comes up or you're more inclined to collapse on the couch than make a meal, canned or frozen produce is a time-saver. You can focus more effort on a salad or entrée and use prepared produce to round out the meal. If you get large bags of frozen veggies, you can take out only what you'll use for a meal, seal up the bag, and store the rest for another time. More and more delicious blends of frozen vegetables are showing up in supermarkets all the time. Canned fruits and veggies are helpful if freezer space is limited, and sometimes canned produce is less expensive than frozen.

Note the expiration dates on canned and frozen items and use older items first. With a few exceptions, "use by" dates don't really mean that the food can no longer be eaten after that time. Manufacturers use these dates to indicate how long a food will be at peak flavor, and they build a margin of safety into their estimates. Be more cautious about using refrigerated items past their "use by" dates, and keep in mind that frozen foods should be eaten within three to six months.

Also know that many cans are lined with bisphenol A (BPA) or bisphenol S (BPS), chemicals that are hormone disrupters and potential carcinogens. Opt for brands labeled "BPA-free," or better yet, purchase foods packaged in glass jars rather than in cans.

Compost and the Single Vegan

When you throw something away, there is no "away"—a place that magically makes unwanted items disappear. Discarding items merely removes them from your sight, but they all go somewhere. The same is true of food scraps and spoiled leftovers. If you keep potted plants, have landscaping, or tend a small garden, turn that food waste into solid gold by making compost. All vegan food can be composted! Keep a small bucket with a tight-fitting lid under your sink or a gallon container with a screw top on your counter to collect scraps. There are many excellent ways to do small-scale composting, even for apartment dwellers. An online search can provide sources for kitchen composters.

COOK BIG, STORE SMALL

Many people don't have the time to make every meal from scratch, and if you're cooking for just yourself, you may be less motivated to whip something up. There are a few strategies you can employ to save time and money but still have access to ready-to-eat foods:

- Cook large quantities and store the leftovers in single-serving containers.
- Make large amounts of beans and grains and store them in the freezer for almost-instant meals.
- Prepare more chopped veggies, gravy, or bread dough than you'll need immediately, and refrigerate or freeze the extras to save time prepping in the future. Be sure not to fill the containers all the way, as foods expand when they're frozen.

Leftovers from nearly all the main-dish recipes in this book make great next-day lunches. To quickly determine which prepared foods will survive well in the freezer, make a note of what's available in the frozen food section of the supermarket. You can also make a sandwich or salad specifically for lunch the next day and save that leftover dinner for a day or two later; this way, you won't get tired of eating the same thing two days in a row. If you're able to bring food from home to eat for lunch at work, set yourself up with a lunch bag and containers that fit well in it. Get in the habit of storing leftovers in those lunch containers so you can grab them and go, without worrying about washing out a container beforehand. If you can, take a few containers with you when you go out to eat and skip the styrofoam takeout boxes many restaurants still use.

It doesn't take a lot of time to cook up a bag of dried beans and freeze individual servings. A fifteen-ounce can of beans contains roughly 1¾ cups. Canned beans are inexpensive, but home-cooked dried beans cost even less, and you can control the amount of salt and other added ingredients in them. If you don't have time to check on a simmering pot of food, invest in a two- or four-quart slow cooker or multifunction programmable pressure cooker. Both of these appliances cut the cooking times for beans, grains, soups, and stews considerably, and the small sizes are likely to fit both your counter space and budget.

Whenever you make rice, millet, quinoa, or other whole grains, prepare enough for several meals and put the extras in single-serving freezer containers. Use the leftover grain in a soup, as the base for a hearty salad or side dish, or as the foundation of a stir-fry or main dish. Alternatively, mix it with beans to create veggie burgers or a filling for burritos.

If you frequently use onion in dishes, chop a few at a time and freeze them in several small containers. You can follow the same procedure for diced bell peppers, sliced jalapeño chiles, and chopped broccoli, carrots, and celery. Cook chopped mushrooms prior to freezing them, as otherwise they won't hold up well.

If you're making a cooked sauce or gravy, prepare a large amount and store single servings in the fridge or freezer. With a sauce or gravy already made, you'll always have a topping for quick meals of whole grains and veggies with beans, tempeh, or tofu.

If you crave the aroma and flavor of freshly baked bread, prepare enough dough for one or two loaves. Divide the dough into small portions (enough to make a roll or two) and freeze each one in an airtight storage container. You can defrost a portion in the fridge overnight or at room temperature in just a few hours and bake fresh rolls for dinner.

Minced fresh garlic perks up any cooked dish. But if you need to save time and don't mind the expense, look for small jars of minced garlic in the produce section of your supermarket. You can often find fresh herbs packed in oil or in squeeze tubes; just be sure all the ingredients in the container are vegan. If you need to save money and have the time, you can always make your own jars of minced garlic and store them in the refrigerator or freezer.

Store flour or corn tortillas in the freezer so they'll stay fresh until you need them. Warm them to make a superquick burrito. Topped with nut butter, they'll make a comforting, nutritious snack, or layer on some hum-

Building a Main-Dish Salad

Think of a main-dish salad as a variation on the traditional stir-fry. A stir-fry will often consist of a protein and stir-fried veggies served over a grain, and the protein, veggies, and grain are usually in equal proportions. A main-dish salad will have a greater proportion of veggies, mostly fresh, served on top of a smaller amount of grain and topped with a little protein. Sometimes the protein or grain will be mixed in with the veggies. Finally, the whole salad is pulled together with a dressing.

There's no right or wrong way to assemble a main-dish salad, and the only limit to what ingredients can be used is your imagination. Although intact whole grains, such as brown rice, millet, and quinoa, are the most nutritious, you could use any shape of whole-grain pasta or make croutons from whole-grain bread. If you're using cooked grains that have been stored in the fridge, you may need to separate the grains with your fingers or a fork to distribute them evenly within the salad. If you use cooked beans, be sure to rinse them well first to remove excess sodium and prevent the bean liquid from competing with the salad dressing. Transform tofu into vegan feta cubes by marinating it in an Italian-style salad dressing or vinaigrette for several hours, then draining.

mus with lettuce and sprouts for a light lunch. Open the package of tortillas and slip pieces of waxed paper between them before freezing so they'll be easy to separate.

Rice paper wraps can transform salad veggies into instant spring rolls. Dip the stiff rice papers one at a time into warm water for a few seconds, just until pliable. Top with a line of veggies down the center, roll up, and eat with your favorite Asian dipping sauce.

WHEN TIME IS OF THE ESSENCE

Some people just can't manage eating breakfast before they have to go to work. If that describes you, don't leave home empty-handed; you'll be hungry soon enough. Prepare one of the smoothies on pages 19–20, pour it into a no-drip insulated drink container, and make room for it in your lunch bag. Cook slices of fried tofu or tempeh in advance, keep a stash of whole-grain English muffins in the fridge, and put together your own breakfast sandwiches.

Take a tightly closed tub of cut fruit or fresh berries and an unopened container or two of your favorite vegan yogurt to mix together once you get to work. Even if you eat breakfast before you leave the house, this makes a great midday snack. If adding a whole banana to the yogurt is too much food for you, cut an unpeeled banana in half and peel it once you're ready to eat it; the unpeeled half will keep just fine until the next day, or you can peel it and freeze it to use in a smoothie (see page 4). Try Overnight Oats with Nut Butter and Berries (page 22). Divide the oats among storage containers, and add fresh fruit and nuts right before you leave in the morning.

Cut up a variety of veggies (such as broccoli, cabbage, carrots, celery, mushrooms, onions, and zucchini) and store them in containers at eye level in the refrigerator. Seeing all those colorful veggies ready to go will inspire you to add them to salads or stir fries more frequently.

Even penny-pinching single vegans are going to have moments when they appreciate having a commercially prepared frozen entrée or two on hand. Although frozen dinners won't measure up to the quality and freshness of something you'd make yourself, an increasing number of manufacturers are including vegan options in their lineup. Companies catering to vegans also tend to be more aware of health and environmental concerns and often make quality products using organic ingredients. Also, it's a good idea to opt for prepared foods that have 140 grams of sodium or less per serving; you can always add a bit more flavoring at the dinner table if you prefer. Faux meats, such as vegan bacon, sausage, and deli slices, are fun to have occasionally, but their sodium content is usually very high, and they often contain undesirable amounts of processed flavorings and preservatives. Fortunately, more food manufacturers are responding to customer demand, and there are now many prepared items, such as veggie burgers, that are made primarily with whole-food ingredients.

Frozen burritos and potpies are typically good choices. Pizza tends to be high in calories and short on veggies, but you can top it with finely chopped broccoli or greens before baking or include a nutritious salad as a side dish.

OTHER MONEY-SAVING SHOPPING TIPS

Look for store brands when you shop for canned and frozen foods and other pantry items. Often the quality is just as good as more expensive brands but at a much lower cost. Take advantage of shelf labels that list the cost per ounce or per item, as this will make price comparison relatively easy.

It almost goes without saying, but here goes: keep track of what you spend, especially if you're establishing your first kitchen. You'll have a better idea if you can splurge or if you need to be more thrifty. Pay particular attention to the prices of items you use often. If they go on sale, you'll be able to tell whether it's worth stocking up on them if you've been monitoring costs.

If you have the money and the space, buy pantry foods in bulk to take advantage of the cost savings. There are several online directories for food-buying clubs, so you can search for one near you. If money and space are in short supply, team up with family members or friends and make bulk purchases together.

You can use the same tactic for group purchases of fresh produce if you buy in bulk and in season; just freeze, can, or store your share. Also consider joining a community supported agriculture program (CSA) so you can purchase locally grown, seasonal fruits and vegetables directly from a farmer in your community. CSAs give consumers a chance to buy an annual "share" of the farm's produce, which helps support the coming year's crops with upfront money for a membership. In return, each week during the growing season, you'll receive a box or bag of fresh, seasonal produce directly from the farm. When you participate in a CSA, you support local farmers (a valuable resource), get veggies at a good price, and occasionally receive unique foods to try. Many CSAs offer "half shares" for smaller households, so be sure to inquire whether that option is available.

Fresh herbs can be expensive, but basil, chives, cilantro, rosemary, savory, and thyme are relatively easy to grow indoors. They do well planted in pots located in a sunny window. If you have space outdoors that gets lots of light, take advantage of the opportunity to grow some of your own produce. Start out in the early spring with a few lettuce or spinach plants in a large container of garden soil. Once the evening temperatures no longer dip below 60 degrees F, you can replace those greens with a single tomato, cucumber, or bell pepper plant. If you're more adventurous, stick some strawberry plants in with your greens; they make good garden companions.

BEST CHOICES FOR TAKEOUT

A steady diet of processed food is never a good idea, especially because most of these items are extremely high in sodium and additives. But organizations such as One Green Planet (onegreenplanet.org) and PETA (peta.org) have lists of healthy vegan fast-food options on their websites. Consult these when you know you'll need to eat out or get takeout.

A number of supermarkets are expanding their deli sections to include whole-grain and plant-based options, and many now carry items such as quinoa and roasted vegetables that would have been difficult to find until recently. If the ingredients in deli foods aren't clearly listed or shown on product tags in the deli case, ask the counter server to provide you with their recipe book or ingredient lists so you can make sure the foods are totally vegan.

I can't say enough about the benefit of having a few foods you can grab and eat just as they are, particularly if you're watching your weight or need to cut back on fat or sodium. It's smart to always keep a few apples, bananas, carrots, peaches or pears, and tomatoes on hand, along with raw nuts and perhaps some of your favorite dried fruit.

GETTING SET UP

f you're setting up a kitchen just for yourself, you really don't need much in the way of equipment and staples. Here are the basics, but feel free to add to this list depending on your needs and how much money and storage space you have.

Essential Tools

By definition, vegans are plant eaters, and nothing encourages the preparation of fresh produce more than having the right knives in your kitchen. A good chef's knife with an eight-inch blade and a sizeable handle is the most important kitchen tool you can own. You can spend a fortune on a knife, but a decent one can be had for under twenty dollars. If you're fortunate enough to have a restaurant supply store nearby, you can get a quality commercial knife fairly inexpensively. Choose a chef's knife that feels comfortable when you hold it by the handle the way you would to cut veggies. Look for one that's substantial and has a bit of heft but isn't too heavy to use. A paring knife is important for cutting smaller fruits and vegetables, and the sharp point can come in handy for tasks such as coring apples. If you love fresh bread, a long, serrated bread knife is essential. The scalloped edges will slice through loaves, fresh pastry, and tomatoes without compressing them. You might also want to get a paring knife with a serrated edge so it can do double duty.

Once you have a few knives, be sure to get either a hardwood or bamboo cutting board. Cutting directly on your countertops will ruin their surfaces and wear down your knives. Wood boards should be conditioned every so often by rubbing them with food-grade mineral oil, which is available at many supermarkets as well as cookware and hardware stores.

You can do all your stove-top cooking with four pans, max: two skillets for frying (eight-inch and ten-inch) and two saucepans (one-quart and three-quart), although a larger saucepan (four-quart or six-quart) can be useful for cooking pasta and soups. Look for stainless steel or porcelain-enamel skillets and saucepans with heavy bottoms, which will help prevent foods from scorching. Unlike other metals (such as aluminum, copper, or iron), stainless steel as well as nonstick porcelain enamel are nonreactive, which means they won't affect the flavor of acidic foods, such as tomato sauce.

Having a couple of eight-inch square or round baking pans, a six-cup muffin pan, an 8 x 4 x 2½-inch loaf pan, and a baking sheet will allow you to make small batches of baked goods. Consider getting a roll of parchment paper to line the bottoms of these and perhaps a silicone baking mat for the baking sheet. They'll prevent foods from sticking and make cleanup a breeze. Even if you don't envision yourself baking breads and desserts, you can use a small baking pan or baking sheet for baking potatoes and putting underneath frozen entrées.

For food prep, treat yourself to a decent can opener. Good ones usually cost only a few dollars more than cheaper versions. Get one that slices around the top of the can rather than through it. That way, you won't be left with a sharp edge, and there's less chance of food seeping up from inside the can into the opener. To complete your food-prep kit, outfit your kitchen with the following:

- Grater
- Measuring cups and spoons
- Metal colander *(with holes, not mesh) for draining beans and pasta*
- Metal spatula *(plus a wooden or bamboo spatula to use on nonstick pans)*
- Mixing bowls *(small, medium, and large)*
- Peeler
- Potato masher *(optional)*
- Silicone spatula/scraper
- Wooden spoons *(one or two for savory foods and one or two for sweet or neutral foods)*

If you're setting up a kitchen for the first time, pick up some small glass storage containers with snap-on lids (although the lids are plastic, they don't have to come in contact with your food). Inexpensive sets are available at most supermarkets or can be purchased online. Once you get cooking, you'll eventually find yourself collecting glass jars with lids from the foods you purchase, and you may never have to buy storage containers again.

Small Appliances

If you have the money and space, consider getting a few countertop appliances that can enhance your foodie experience. (See the information on slow cookers and pressure cookers on page 8.) The first splurge I'd recommend is a personal blender. They're available in a variety of sizes and price ranges, but you'll probably get the most use out of one that costs between sixty and eighty dollars. Some brands come with drink lids for the blender containers, so you can make a smoothie and sip it on the go. The smaller blender containers are great for whipping up salad dressings and even grinding flaxseeds.

If you're on a tight budget, you should be able to find a decent traditional blender for less than the cost of a personal blender. They take up a bit more space on the counter, and you'll have to transfer food from the blender jar into another container every time you use it. Go with a basic model. You don't need a dozen different blending speeds; the fewer buttons, the better. If you're regularly making nut butters or hummus, it would be worth investing in a high-powered blender, as the motors in inexpensive, low-powered models may burn out trying to get the job done. Some high-powered blenders are designed to fit on counters underneath upper cabinets so you don't have to store them after use. Look for factory-reconditioned models, as they typically come with warranties and are in like-new condition, but their price tags tend to be much lower than new machines.

If you have the budget and space for both a modest blender and another appliance, a food processor is an alternative to a high-powered blender. Food processors are built to accommodate the thick, dry mixtures that conventional blenders struggle with, and they're relatively inexpensive.

A toaster oven is incredibly handy, and if you can afford it, get one with baking options (such as variable temperature settings and timers) similar to conventional ovens. As a solo vegan, you'll probably want to bake just a couple of potatoes at a time or heat up a single roll or frozen entrée. Although a toaster oven might not accomplish these tasks any faster than a large oven, it will preheat quickly, so it will use less electricity and will eventually pay for itself.

To microwave or not is a matter of personal preference. Some people don't trust the technology further than they can throw it, while others can't imagine living without it. If you do go the microwave route, there's no need to invest in one that will hold anything larger than a dinner plate. Remember that veggies will cook more evenly in a microwave if they're uniform in size, and use glass or ceramic containers for microwaving foods instead of plastic.

Foods to Have on Hand

Everyone's needs and preferences are unique, so what you have in your pantry will be unique as well. However, below are recommendations for some staples that are fundamental for almost every vegan. You could make many meals just from this list. Included are optional items you might also need for making some of the recipes in this book.

PACKAGED STAPLES	OPTIONAL PACKAGED STAPLES	CANNED GOODS	FROZEN FOODS	SEASONINGS
Agave nectar	Cacao powder or cocoa powder	Corn	Baked goods (bread, English muffins, rolls, tortillas)	Chili powder
Baking powder	Chocolate chips, vegan	Pasta sauce	Bananas (peeled whole)	Curry powder
Baking soda	Coconut, unsweetened shredded dried	Tomato sauce	Berries	Garlic powder
Beans, canned and dried	Couscous	Tomatoes (crushed or diced)	Broccoli	Onion powder
Brown rice	Maple syrup		Corn	Vanilla extract
Coffee	Millet	**REFRIGERATED FOODS**	Edamame	
Dried fruit	Nuts (almonds, Brazil nuts, pecans, or walnuts)	Butter, vegan	Green beans	**OPTIONAL SEASONINGS**
Flour (all-purpose, whole wheat, or whole wheat pastry)	Quinoa	Condiments (ketchup, vegan mayo, mustard, sriracha sauce)	Peas	Basil, dried
Nut butter (almond or peanut butter)	Seeds (chia, hemp, sesame, or sunflower)	Flaxseed oil	Spinach	Cayenne
Oil (olive or sunflower)	Sugar, granulated (unbleached cane, brown, or coconut)	Milk, nondairy	**OPTIONAL FROZEN FOODS**	Cinnamon, ground
Pasta (your favorite kinds)	Toasted sesame oil	Tempeh	Berries and other fruits in season	Coriander, ground
Popcorn		Tofu	Brussels sprouts	Cumin, ground
Rolled oats		**OPTIONAL REFRIGERATED FOODS**	California mixed vegetables (broccoli, carrots, and cauliflower)	Ginger, ground
Salt		Cheese, nondairy		Hot sauce
Seed butter (sunflower butter or tahini)		Miso	Edamame	Italian seasoning
Tamari		Sausages, vegan	Mixed vegetables (carrots, corn, green beans, and peas)	Nutmeg, ground
Tea		Seitan		Nutritional yeast flakes
Vegetable broth		Sour cream, nondairy		Oregano, dried
Vinegar (balsamic or cider vinegar)		Yogurt, nondairy		Paprika, sweet or smoked
				Poultry seasoning
				Red pepper flakes, crushed
				Thyme, dried
				Turmeric, ground

MENUS FOR ONE

The following menus will give you a week's worth of great meals without repetition. If you prefer, substitute leftovers from a previous dinner for any lunch. If you use leftovers for lunch, you can replace the dinner suggestion with the lunch choice from that day. Any of the sweet snack recipes will yield enough to provide light desserts for you to enjoy after lunch or dinner.

a week of menus for one

	BREAKFAST	LUNCH	SNACK	DINNER
MON	Green Detox Smoothie, page 20	sandwich made with No Yolks Egg Salad, page 76	Raw Energy Balls, page 122	Curried Lentils with Spinach, page 104; Indian-Style Millet, page 94
TUE	Overnight Oats with Nut Butter and Berries, page 22	Tomato-Vegetable Soup, page 62; Hummus and Veggie Wrap, page 71	fresh fruit with optional vegan yogurt	Tuscan Tempeh with Onion and Bell Pepper, page 105; Garlicky Greens, page 85; Wheat Bread or Rolls, page 136
WED	Avocado Toast with Tomato, page 23	Vegan Split Pea and Bacon Soup, page 65; Classic BLT, page 77	Oatmeal Raisin Cookies, page 118	Nutty Bulgur-Stuffed Peppers, page 109; California Vegetables au Gratin, page 90
THU	Banana-Berry Smoothie Bowl, page 21	Thirty-Minute Chili, page 66; Cornbread, page 135	Seasoned and Seeded Kale Chips, page 36	Versatile Veggie-Bean Burgers, page 78; Baked French Fries or Wedges, page 91
FRI	Tex-Mex Breakfast Burritos, page 26	Roasted Butternut Bisque, page 64; Berry and Melon Salad with Agave-Lime Dressing, page 50	fresh fruit with optional vegan yogurt	Personal Pita Pizza, page 115; Veggie Chef's Salad, page 57; Mini Cashew Cheesecakes, page 142
SAT	Maple, Apple, and Pecan Waffles, page 30	Waldorf Salad with Yogurt Dressing, page 51	Strawberry-Banana Soft-Serve Ice Cream, page 127	Barbecue Tofu or Tempeh, page 114; Classic Coleslaw, page 58; Mac-n-Cheese, page 113
SUN	Breakfast Potato-and-Veggie Skillet, page 25	Loaded Bean Burritos, page 72	Baked Apples, page 138	Seitan and Veggie Stew, page 68; Drop Biscuits, page 134

ABOUT THE RECIPES

Most of the recipes in this book are fairly easy to make and call for just a few ingredients that are readily available in most supermarkets. You'll find everything from must-have basics to fun-to-put-together dishes when you want to treat yourself. Variations are included, so you can learn how to customize recipes with your favorite ingredients or flavors.

Most of the recipes yield one or two servings, so you can occasionally have enough left over for another meal. Small-quantity baked goods are easy to make and will provide treats you can dig into right now, along with a few extras you can freeze and enjoy another time. It's also easy to prepare two to four servings of soups or stews, and because their flavors deepen after a day or two, these recipes are designed to leave you with enough for additional meals.

When you're trying out a new recipe, read it over thoroughly before you dive in. Make sure you have all the ingredients on hand and understand all the instructions. Unless an optional ingredient is suggested, wait to make substitutions until you've had a chance to try out the recipe as it was originally written. Then, next time, you can make changes to suit your personal preferences or incorporate the ingredients you have available.

CHAPTER TWO

Breakfast Ideas

Berry Red Smoothie

Red smoothies are the latest craze for jump-starting weight loss, reducing inflammation in the body, and improving overall health. This luscious libation is made with red vegetables, fruits, and juice. For an energizing boost, add the optional chia seeds or maca or cacao powders.

MAKES 1 SERVING

Per serving:

272 calories

9 g protein

3 g fat (0 g sat)

78 g carbs

77 mg sodium

140 mg calcium

16 g fiber

1   small red beet, peeled and coarsely chopped

¾   cup pomegranate or grape juice

½   cup hulled and sliced fresh strawberries, or ¾ cup frozen whole strawberries

½   cup fresh or frozen raspberries

½   cup coarsely chopped red bell pepper

½   teaspoon vanilla extract

½   cup ice cubes (optional if using frozen berries)

1   tablespoon maca powder (optional)

1   teaspoon cacao powder (optional)

1   teaspoon chia seeds (optional)

1. Put the beet, pomegranate juice, strawberries, raspberries, bell pepper, and vanilla extract in a blender. Add the optional ice cubes, maca powder, cacao powder, and chia seeds and process until smooth.

2. Pour into a tall glass. Serve immediately.

Green Detox Smoothie

MAKES 1 SERVING

Per serving:

313 calories

6 g protein

8 g fat (0 g sat)

55 g carbs

675 mg sodium

330 mg calcium

2 g fiber

This flavorful smoothie is made with a blend of pineapple, celery, cucumber, and leafy greens, plus tongue-tingling ginger, cayenne, and your choice of lemon or lime. All these fruits and veggies are beneficial for detoxifying the body and improving your immunity.

1   **cup stemmed leafy greens** (such as spinach or kale), lightly packed

⅔   **cup plain nondairy milk**

⅔   **cup fresh, canned, or frozen pineapple chunks**

½   **cup coarsely chopped cucumber**

1   **stalk celery, coarsely chopped**

½   **cup ice cubes**

Juice of 1 lemon (¼ cup) **or lime** (2 tablespoons)

1   **tablespoon peeled and grated fresh ginger**

Pinch cayenne

2   **tablespoons hemp seeds** (optional)

1   **teaspoon chia seeds** (optional)

1. Put the leafy greens, milk, pineapple, cucumber, celery, ice cubes, lemon juice, ginger, and cayenne in a blender. Add the optional hemp seeds and chia seeds and process until smooth.

2. Pour into a tall glass. Serve immediately.

Banana-Berry Smoothie Bowl

Eat a smoothie with a spoon rather than sip it through a straw! Affectionately called smoothie bowls, spoonable smoothies are fun alternatives to cereal for breakfast. This one features a smoothie base made with banana, almond milk, and flaxseeds, and it's decorated with additional banana slices, berries, and crunchy toppings.

MAKES 1 SERVING

Per serving:

400 calories

10 g protein

16 g fat (2 g sat)

62 g carbs

150 mg sodium

390 mg calcium

9 g fiber

⅔ cup plain or vanilla almond milk or other nondairy milk

1 large banana, thinly sliced

1 tablespoon nut or seed butter (such as almond, hazelnut, peanut, or sunflower butter)

2 teaspoons ground flaxseeds or flaxseed meal

½ teaspoon vanilla extract

⅓ cup fresh or frozen berries (such as blueberries, blackberries, raspberries, or sliced strawberries), **thawed**

¼ cup granola, or 2 tablespoons sliced almonds and 1 tablespoon unsweetened dried shredded coconut

1. Put the milk, half the sliced banana, and the nut butter, flaxseeds, and vanilla extract in a blender and process until smooth. The mixture should be very thick, with a consistency similar to soft-serve ice cream.

2. Transfer to a bowl. Decoratively arrange the remaining banana slices, berries, and granola on top. Serve immediately.

GREEN SMOOTHIE BOWL: Add 1 cup stemmed leafy greens, lightly packed, to the blender.

VARIATION: Replace the smoothie portion of this recipe with any of the other smoothie recipes in this chapter.

Overnight Oats with Nut Butter and Berries

MAKES 1 SERVING

Per serving:

368 calories

9 g protein

18 g fat (2 g sat)

49 g carbs

126 mg sodium

590 mg calcium

10 g fiber

For an effortless but satisfying breakfast, overnight oats are the answer. Oats can be softened simply by soaking them in nondairy milk and yogurt for eight to twelve hours in the refrigerator. The result? A creamy, instant breakfast cereal.

1   container (6 ounces) **plain or vanilla vegan yogurt**

½   **cup plain or vanilla nondairy milk**

⅓   **cup old-fashioned rolled oats**

1   **tablespoon nut or seed butter** (such as almond, hazelnut, peanut, or sunflower butter)

½   **teaspoon vanilla extract**

½   **cup fresh or frozen berries** (such as blueberries, blackberries, or raspberries), **thawed**

1. Put the yogurt, milk, oats, nut butter, and vanilla extract in a small bowl and stir to combine. Cover and refrigerate for 8 to 12 hours.

2. Stir well, then top with the berries. Serve immediately.

TO-GO TIP

Prepare the oats in a small, airtight container.

Avocado Toast with Tomato

Move over, margarine and jam. There's a new toast topper in town, and it may surprise you. In the time it takes to toast the bread, you can create a creamy spread by mashing an avocado with a little lemon juice and seasonings. It tastes even better with a diced tomato on top.

> 1   avocado, diced
> Juice of ½ lemon (2 tablespoons)
> Sea salt
> Crushed red pepper flakes
> 2   slices whole-grain bread or other bread, toasted
> 1   Roma tomato, diced

1. Put the avocado and lemon juice in a small bowl and mash with a fork until as smooth and creamy as you like. Season with salt and red pepper flakes to taste.

2. Spread the avocado mixture on the toasted bread, then top with the tomato. Serve immediately.

MAKES 2 SLICES, 1 SERVING

Per serving:
387 calories
8 g protein
23 g fat (3 g sat)
43 g carbs
283 mg sodium
260 mg calcium
13 g fiber

Note: Analysis doesn't include sea salt and crushed red pepper flakes to taste.

Spiced Apple-Walnut Roll-Up

To create this fast and filling breakfast roll-up, tender slices of sautéed and spiced apple and walnuts are encased in a flour tortilla that's drizzled with maple syrup.

1   large apple, coarsely chopped

3   tablespoons coarsely chopped walnuts

1   tablespoon vegan butter

1   tablespoon maple syrup, plus more for drizzling

¼   teaspoon ground cinnamon

½   teaspoon vanilla extract

1   (8-inch or larger) **flour tortilla**

1. Put the apple, walnuts, and butter in a large nonstick skillet and cook over medium heat, stirring occasionally, until the apple is tender, 3 to 5 minutes.

2. Add the maple syrup and cinnamon and stir to combine. Decrease the heat to low and cook, stirring occasionally, for 1 minute. Add the vanilla extract and stir to combine. Transfer to a small bowl.

3. For easier rolling, warm the tortilla in a large nonstick skillet over medium heat, 1 minute per side. Alternatively, microwave the tortilla for 20 to 30 seconds.

4. To assemble, put the tortilla on a large plate and spoon the apple mixture in the center of it. Fold the bottom half of the tortilla over the filling and continue rolling it over like a crêpe. Drizzle additional maple syrup over the top if desired. Serve immediately.

VARIATION: Replace the apple with 1 large pear, peach, or nectarine, coarsely chopped.

Breakfast Potato-and-Veggie Skillet

Grab a potato, dice it, and cook it in a skillet along with onion, bell pepper, and kale to create this substantial breakfast. It's especially delicious topped with hot sauce or salsa.

MAKES 1 SERVING

Per serving:

403 calories

19 g protein

16 g fat (3 g sat)

66 g carbs

362 mg sodium

250 mg calcium

15 g fiber

Note: Analysis doesn't include sea salt and freshly ground black pepper to taste.

1   potato, peeled and cut into ½-inch cubes

2   teaspoons olive oil or other oil

⅓   cup diced red or yellow onion

⅓   cup diced red bell pepper

2   large leaves kale, stemmed and cut into thin strips

1½ teaspoons nutritional yeast flakes

1   teaspoon Italian seasoning

¼   teaspoon sweet or smoked paprika

Sea salt

Freshly ground black pepper

¼   cup shredded vegan Cheddar cheese

1. Put the potato and oil a large nonstick skillet and cook over medium heat, stirring occasionally, for 5 minutes.

2. Add the onion and bell pepper and cook, stirring occasionally, for 3 minutes.

3. Add the kale, nutritional yeast, Italian seasoning, and paprika and cook, stirring occasionally, until the kale is wilted and the potato is tender, 3 to 5 minutes.

4. Season with salt and pepper to taste. Scatter the cheese over the top. Serve hot.

Tex-Mex Breakfast Burritos

For these burritos, tofu is crumbled into bite-sized pieces, seasoned, and cooked in a skillet much like scrambled eggs. Next, shredded vegan cheese and salsa are added, and then everything is rolled up in flour tortillas to create a hearty burrito breakfast.

SCRAMBLED TOFU

8   ounces firm or extra-firm tofu

1   tablespoon nutritional yeast flakes

½   teaspoon garlic powder

¼   teaspoon onion powder

¼   teaspoon sweet or smoked paprika, or ¼ teaspoon chili powder

⅛   teaspoon ground turmeric (optional)

Sea salt

Freshly ground black pepper

TORTILLAS AND TOPPINGS

2   (8-inch or larger) **flour tortillas**

4   tablespoons shredded vegan Cheddar cheese

6   tablespoons Avocado and Black Bean Salsa (page 32), or 4 tablespoons salsa

1. To make the scrambled tofu, lightly oil a large nonstick skillet or mist it with cooking spray. Heat over medium-high heat.

2. Using your fingers, crumble the tofu into the hot skillet. Sprinkle the nutritional yeast, garlic powder, onion powder, paprika, and optional turmeric over the top and cook, stirring occasionally, until hot and starting to brown, 3 to 5 minutes. Season with salt and pepper to taste.

3. For easier rolling, warm each tortilla in a large nonstick skillet over medium heat, 1 minute per side. Alternatively, microwave the tortillas for 20 to 30 seconds.

4. To assemble, put one tortilla on a large plate. Spoon half the tofu in the center of it and top with half the cheese and half the salsa.

5. To roll the burrito, fold the bottom half of the tortilla over the filling, fold in each side toward the center over the filling, and roll up from the bottom edge to enclose the filling.

SAVE FOR LATER

Stored seam-side down in an airtight container, the extra burrito will keep for 2 days in the refrigerator.

TO-GO TIP

Put the burrito seam-side down in an airtight container.

6. Put the burrito seam-side down on a plate. Repeat the process with the remaining tortilla, tofu, cheese, and salsa. Serve immediately.

Buttermilk Pancakes

Nondairy milk is combined with a little cider vinegar to make a vegan version of buttermilk, which is combined with a few pantry staples to create these light and fluffy pancakes. Serve them with your choice of toppings, such as vegan butter, maple syrup, or agave nectar.

⅔ cup plain or vanilla nondairy milk

2 teaspoons cider vinegar

⅔ cup unbleached all-purpose flour or whole wheat pastry flour

1½ teaspoons baking powder

½ teaspoon ground cinnamon

¼ teaspoon sea salt

1 tablespoon sunflower oil or other oil

1 tablespoon maple syrup or agave nectar

½ teaspoon vanilla extract

1. Put the milk and vinegar in a small bowl and stir to combine. Let rest for 5 minutes to thicken.

2. Put the flour, baking powder, cinnamon, and salt in a medium bowl and whisk to combine.

3. Add the milk mixture, oil, maple syrup, and vanilla extract to the flour mixture and whisk until just combined. A few lumps are fine, but don't overmix or the pancakes will be tough. Let the batter rest for 5 minutes.

4. Lightly oil a large nonstick skillet or griddle or mist it with cooking spray. Heat over medium heat.

5. When the skillet is hot, portion the batter into it using ⅓ cup of batter for each pancake. Cook until the edges of the pancakes are dry and the bottoms are lightly browned, 3 to 4 minutes. Flip the pancakes over and cook until lightly browned on the other side, 2 to 3 minutes.

6. Lightly oil the skillet between batches and repeat with the remaining batter. Serve hot.

SAVE FOR LATER

Stored in an airtight container, the extra pancakes will keep for 3 days in the refrigerator. Warm in a skillet over low heat before serving.

BUCKWHEAT BUTTERMILK PANCAKES: Replace the unbleached all-purpose flour with ⅓ cup buckwheat flour and ⅓ cup brown rice or white rice flour.

Maple, Apple, and Pecan Waffles

**MAKES 2 WAFFLES,
2 SERVINGS**

Per serving:

235 calories

3 g protein

14 g fat (4 g sat)

30 g carbs

555 mg sodium

130 mg calcium

3 g fiber

The ideal waffles are crispy on the outside and chewy on the inside, and this is easily accomplished by adding a little cornmeal to the batter. You get a taste of autumn in each bite of these nutty, applesauce-flavored waffles. Serve them with your choice of toppings, such as vegan butter, maple syrup, or agave nectar.

⅓ cup plain or vanilla nondairy milk

½ teaspoon cider vinegar

⅓ cup applesauce

2 tablespoons maple syrup

1½ teaspoons coconut oil, melted, or other oil

½ teaspoon vanilla extract

⅔ cup unbleached all-purpose flour

2 tablespoons fine or medium-grind cornmeal

1 teaspoon baking powder

¾ teaspoon ground cinnamon

½ teaspoon baking soda

⅛ teaspoon sea salt

¼ cup finely chopped pecans or walnuts

1. Put the milk and vinegar in a small bowl and stir to combine. Let rest for 5 minutes to thicken.

2. Add the applesauce, maple syrup, oil, and vanilla extract and stir to combine.

3. Put the flour, cornmeal, baking powder, cinnamon, baking soda, and salt in a medium bowl and whisk to combine.

4. Add the milk mixture and whisk until just combined. Gently stir in the pecans.

5. Preheat a waffle iron according to the manufacturer's instructions. When the waffle iron is hot, lightly oil or mist it with cooking spray.

6. Depending on the size of your waffle iron, ladle ¾ to 1 cup of batter onto the iron and cook according to the manufacturer's instructions or until golden brown.

7. Repeat the process with the remaining batter. Serve hot.

SAVE FOR LATER

Stored in an airtight container, the extra waffle will keep for 3 days in the refrigerator. Warm in a skillet over low heat before serving.

Snacks

Avocado and Black Bean Salsa

**MAKES 1½ CUPS,
3 SERVINGS**

Per serving:

136 calories

4 g protein

8 g fat (1 g sat)

13 g carbs

6 mg sodium

20 mg calcium

6 g fiber

*Note: Analysis doesn't include
sea salt and freshly ground black
pepper to taste.*

Creamy cubes of avocado and cooked black beans are combined with tomato, onion, bell pepper, and jalapeño chile to create this chunky salsa. Dig in with your favorite tortilla chips, add it to your favorite burrito filling, or spoon it over your favorite Mexican or Southwestern dishes.

1	Roma tomato, diced
⅓	cup diced orange or yellow bell pepper
¼	cup diced yellow onion
1	green onion, thinly sliced
2	tablespoons chopped fresh cilantro

Juice of 1 lime (2 tablespoons)

½	jalapeño chile, seeded and finely diced
2	large cloves garlic, minced
1	avocado, diced
½	cup cooked or canned black beans, drained and rinsed

Sea salt

Freshly ground black pepper

1. Put the tomato, bell pepper, onion, green onion, cilantro, lime juice, chile, and garlic in a medium bowl and stir to combine.
2. Add the avocado and black beans and gently stir to combine. Season with salt and pepper to taste.

BLACK BEAN AND CORN SALSA: Replace the avocado with ½ cup canned corn, drained and rinsed, or frozen corn kernels, thawed.

SAVE FOR LATER

Stored in an airtight container, the salsa will keep for 3 days in the refrigerator.

Zesty Guacamole

For the best-tasting guacamole, it's important to use a fully ripened avocado, so buy one a few days before you plan to make a batch of this dip. To amplify the flavor, mash the chile, onion, garlic, lime juice, and seasonings together before adding the avocado to the mix. Serve the guacamole as a dip or top your favorite dishes with it.

**MAKES ¾ CUP,
3 SERVINGS**

Per serving:

109 calories

7 g protein

1 g fat (1 g sat)

9 g carbs

8 mg sodium

0 mg calcium

5 g fiber

Note: Analysis doesn't include sea salt and freshly ground black pepper to taste.

2   tablespoons finely diced red or yellow onion

½   serrano or jalapeño chile, seeded and finely diced

2   large cloves garlic, minced

Juice of ½ lime (1 tablespoon)

1½   teaspoons nutritional yeast flakes

⅛   teaspoon chili powder or hot sauce

1   avocado, cut in half

Sea salt

Freshly ground black pepper

1. Put the onion, chile, garlic, lime juice, nutritional yeast, and chili powder in a medium bowl and mash with a fork or potato masher for 1 minute.

2. Using a spoon, scoop the avocado out of its skin directly into the bowl. Mash with a fork or potato masher to the desired consistency. Season with salt and pepper to taste.

CHUNKY GUACAMOLE: After mashing in the avocado, add ¼ cup diced tomato and 2 tablespoons chopped fresh cilantro. Stir to combine.

SAVE FOR LATER

Stored in an airtight container, the guacamole will keep for 3 days in the refrigerator.

Hummus

**MAKES 1½ CUPS,
4 SERVINGS**

Per serving:

178 calories

8 g protein

10 g fat (1 g sat)

19 g carbs

555 mg sodium

40 mg calcium

6 g fiber

Hands down, hummus is one of the most popular Middle Eastern dips. It's made from chickpeas that are blended with lemon juice, olive oil, and creamy tahini. Serve this versatile dip with pita bread, crackers, or raw vegetables, or use it as a filling for wraps or sandwiches.

1   can (15 ounces) **chickpeas, drained and rinsed**

4   large cloves garlic

3   tablespoons lemon juice

2   tablespoons tahini

1   tablespoon olive oil

½   teaspoon ground cumin

½   teaspoon sea salt

Sweet or smoked paprika, for garnish

1. Put the chickpeas and garlic in a food processor and process for 1 minute.

2. Add the lemon juice, tahini, oil, cumin, and salt and process until completely smooth. Scrape down the work bowl and process for 15 seconds longer.

3. Sprinkle a little paprika over the top before serving if desired.

CURRY-CILANTRO HUMMUS: Add ½ teaspoon curry powder and ¼ cup chopped fresh cilantro, lightly packed, and process with the other ingredients.

OLIVE HUMMUS: Add ⅔ cup pitted green or black olives and process with the other ingredients.

ROASTED RED PEPPER HUMMUS: Bake 1 large red bell pepper at 450 degrees F for 8 to 10 minutes, or until soft. Let cool slightly, remove the seeds and stem, and process with the other ingredients.

SAVE FOR LATER

Stored in an airtight container, the hummus will keep for 1 week in the refrigerator.

Baba Ganoush

Oven-roasted eggplant and garlic are blended with tahini, olive oil, lemon juice, mint, and ground cumin, which adds a slightly smoky flavor to this Middle Eastern classic. Serve it as a dip with raw vegetables, crackers, or pita bread, or use it as a spread for sandwiches.

1   **medium eggplant** (about 1 pound)

2   **large cloves garlic**

Juice of ½ lemon (2 tablespoons)

1½ **tablespoons tahini**

1   **tablespoon chopped fresh mint or parsley**

2   **teaspoons olive oil, plus additional for drizzling**

½   **teaspoon ground cumin**

Sea salt

Freshly ground black pepper

Smoked or sweet paprika, for garnish

1. Preheat the oven to 425 degrees F. Line a baking sheet with parchment paper or a silicone baking mat.

2. Cut the eggplant in half lengthwise and cut several slits into the flesh. Put it cut-side down on the lined baking sheet. Bake for 30 minutes.

3. Put the garlic cloves on the baking sheet with the eggplant. Bake for 5 to 10 minutes longer, or until the garlic is lightly browned and the eggplant is very soft and begins to collapse. Remove from the oven and let cool for 5 minutes.

4. Using a spoon, scoop the eggplant flesh into a food processor. Add the roasted garlic, lemon juice, tahini, mint, oil, and cumin and process until smooth. Scrape down the work bowl and process for 15 seconds longer. Season with salt and pepper to taste.

5. Drizzle with a little olive oil and sprinkle with paprika before serving if desired.

MAKES 1 CUP, 3 SERVINGS

Per serving:

146 calories

5 g protein

12 g fat (2 g sat)

12 g carbs

6 mg sodium

40 mg calcium

7 g fiber

Note: Analysis doesn't include sea salt and freshly ground black pepper to taste.

SAVE FOR LATER

Stored in an airtight container, the baba ganoush will keep for 1 week in the refrigerator.

Seasoned and Seeded Kale Chips

**MAKES 6 CUPS,
4 SERVINGS**

Per serving:

131 calories

7 g protein

9 g fat (1 g sat)

4 g carbs

183 mg sodium

80 mg calcium

9 g fiber

Got kale? Then it's the perfect time to whip up a batch of light and crispy kale chips, which make a delicious, nutritious snack. Leftover chips or very small pieces can be lightly crushed and sprinkled over popcorn, salads, or other dishes to add a healthy boost of flavor and color.

1	bunch (1 pound) curly or Tuscan kale, stemmed and torn into large chip-sized pieces
1½	tablespoons olive oil
1	tablespoon reduced-sodium tamari
1	teaspoon onion powder
1	teaspoon chili powder
1	teaspoon garlic powder
2	tablespoons nutritional yeast flakes
2	tablespoons hemp seeds

1. Using a salad spinner, thoroughly spin-dry the kale in batches. Alternatively, pat the kale with a clean towel or paper towels until it's thoroughly dry. Put the kale in a large bowl.

2. Put the oil, tamari, onion powder, chili powder, and garlic powder in a small bowl and whisk to combine. Drizzle over the kale.

3. Gently massage the kale with your hands until it's evenly coated. Sprinkle the nutritional yeast and hemp seeds over the top and gently massage them into the kale until evenly distributed.

4. Preheat the oven to 300 degrees F. Line two large baking sheets with parchment paper or silicone baking mats and arrange the kale on them in a single layer. Bake for 30 to 40 minutes, turning the pieces over every 15 minutes, until the kale is light and crispy.

5. Cool completely before storing.

SAVE FOR LATER

Stored in an airtight container, the kale chips will keep for 1 week at room temperature.

TIP: To dehydrate the chips instead of baking them, arrange the kale in a single layer on three or four dehydrator racks. Dehydrate for 4 to 6 hours, until the kale is light and crispy.

Sweet Cinnamon Baked Tortilla Chips

When you're in the mood for something sweet and crunchy, bake up a batch of these sweet tortilla chips coated with cinnamon sugar. Enjoy them as is or dip them into Mango Salsa (page 86). For an extra-special treat, crumble them over a bowl of nondairy ice cream.

MAKES 12 CHIPS, 2 SERVINGS

Per serving:

233 calories

3 g protein

9 g fat (3 g sat)

34 g carbs

277 mg sodium

70 mg calcium

0 g fiber

2   tablespoons unbleached cane sugar

½   teaspoon ground cinnamon

4   teaspoons vegan butter

2   (8-inch) flour tortillas

1. Preheat the oven to 400 degrees F. Line a baking sheet with parchment paper or a silicone baking mat.

2. Put the sugar and cinnamon in a small bowl and stir to combine.

3. Put the butter in a small glass or ceramic bowl and microwave until melted, 20 to 30 seconds. Alternatively, put the butter in a small saucepan and warm over low heat until melted.

4. Put the tortillas on a cutting board. Brush one side of each tortilla with half the melted butter. Evenly sprinkle half the cinnamon-sugar mixture (about 1 tablespoon) over each tortilla. Cut each tortilla into six wedges and arrange them in a single layer on the lined baking sheet.

5. Bake for 5 to 7 minutes, or until light and crispy. Cool completely before storing.

SAVE FOR LATER

Stored in an airtight container, the tortilla chips will keep for 1 week at room temperature.

Sauces and Gravies

CHAPTER **FOUR**

Dark Chocolate Sauce

Using a combination of cacao powder and chocolate chips gives this sauce a rich, dark chocolate flavor, which is sure to please any chocoholic. This sauce makes an excellent topping for nondairy ice cream, cakes, and desserts.

MAKES ¾ CUP, 3 SERVINGS

Per serving:

184 calories

3 g protein

7 g fat (4 g sat)

31 g carbs

35 mg sodium

110 mg calcium

4 g fiber

3	tablespoons cacao powder or unsweetened cocoa powder
1	tablespoon cornstarch or arrowroot
⅔	cup plain or vanilla nondairy milk
2	tablespoons agave nectar
¼	cup vegan chocolate chips
½	teaspoon vanilla extract
	Pinch sea salt

1. Put the cacao powder and cornstarch in a small saucepan and whisk to combine.

2. Add the milk and agave nectar and cook over medium heat, whisking occasionally, until thickened, 1 to 2 minutes.

3. Remove from the heat. Add the chocolate chips, vanilla extract, and salt and whisk until the chocolate chips are melted. Serve warm or at room temperature.

MINT CHOCOLATE SAUCE: When adding the vanilla extract, also add ⅛ teaspoon peppermint extract.

SAVE FOR LATER

Stored in an airtight container, the chocolate sauce will keep for 1 week in the refrigerator. Bring to room temperature or warm in a small saucepan over low heat before serving.

Pesto

**MAKES 1 CUP,
8 SERVINGS**

Per serving:
67 calories
2 g protein
6 g fat (1 g sat)
1 g carbs
110 mg sodium
0 mg calcium
1 g fiber

Fresh herbs, such as basil, are plentiful during the summer months, and that's the ideal season to make pesto. Note that buttery pine nuts can be a tad pricey, so if they're beyond the range of your budget, feel free to substitute walnuts, which have a comparable flavor but are generally much less expensive.

2	cups fresh basil leaves, lightly packed
¼	cup pine nuts or walnuts, lightly toasted
2	tablespoons nutritional yeast flakes
2	tablespoons olive oil
2	large cloves garlic
½	teaspoon sea salt
⅛	teaspoon freshly ground black pepper

1. Put all the ingredients in a food processor and process for 1 minute.

2. Scrape down the work bowl and process for 15 seconds longer.

SPINACH-PARSLEY PESTO: Replace the basil with 1½ cups baby spinach, lightly packed, and ¼ cup fresh Italian parsley leaves, lightly packed.

SUN-DRIED TOMATO-BASIL PESTO: Decrease the amount of basil to ⅔ cup. Soak ½ cup whole sun-dried tomatoes in ⅔ cup warm water until soft. Add both the sun-dried tomatoes and their soaking liquid to the food processor.

SAVE FOR LATER

Stored in an airtight container, the pesto will keep for 1 week in the refrigerator. The pesto can also be portioned and frozen. Line a baking sheet with parchment or waxed paper and spoon the pesto on it in portions of 2 to 4 tablespoons. Freeze until solid. Stored in an airtight container, the pesto portions will keep for 3 months in the freezer.

Spicy Peanut Sauce

Peanut butter can be used for more than just sandwiches and cookies. One taste of this spicy peanut sauce and you'll appreciate the savory possibilities that peanut butter has to offer. The sauce makes a delicious topping for cooked vegetables, noodles, grains, tempeh or tofu, and even salads.

MAKES ¾ CUP, 6 SERVINGS

Per serving:

105 calories

3 g protein

11 g fat (1 g sat)

7 g carbs

222 mg sodium

0 mg calcium

2 g fiber

¼ cup creamy peanut butter

¼ cup coconut water or water

2 tablespoons reduced-sodium tamari

Zest and juice of 1 lime (2 teaspoons zest and 2 tablespoons juice)

2 teaspoons toasted sesame oil

2 teaspoons coconut sugar or light brown sugar

2 large cloves garlic

1 (1-inch) piece fresh ginger, peeled

¼ teaspoon crushed red pepper flakes

¼ teaspoon freshly ground black pepper

1. Put all the ingredients in a blender and process until smooth.

2. Serve warm, cold, or at room temperature. For a warm sauce, transfer to a small saucepan and cook over medium heat, stirring constantly, just until heated through, 1 to 2 minutes.

PEANUT DRESSING: Add an additional 2 tablespoons coconut water or water. Decrease the amount of crushed red pepper flakes to ⅛ teaspoon or omit.

SAVE FOR LATER

Stored in an airtight container, the peanut sauce will keep for 1 week in the refrigerator.

Stir-Fry Sauce

**MAKES ½ CUP,
4 SERVINGS**

Per serving:
77 calories
1 g protein
4 g fat (1 g sat)
9 g carbs
254 mg sodium
0 mg calcium
1 g fiber

Slightly sweet, sour, and salty, this stir-fry sauce hits all the right notes. Keep some on hand to quickly pump up the flavor of stir-fries, steamed veggies, and cooked grains or noodles.

3	tablespoons low-sodium vegetable broth
2	tablespoons reduced-sodium tamari
1	tablespoon brown rice vinegar or cider vinegar
1	tablespoon toasted sesame oil
2	teaspoons agave nectar
2	large cloves garlic, minced
1	(1-inch) piece fresh ginger, peeled and grated
2	teaspoons cornstarch or arrowroot
¼	teaspoon crushed red pepper flakes
⅛	teaspoon freshly ground black pepper

1. Put all the ingredients in a small saucepan and whisk to combine.
2. Cook over medium heat, whisking occasionally, until the sauce thickens, 1 to 2 minutes.
3. Remove from the heat. Use immediately or let cool completely before storing.

SESAME-GINGER DRESSING: Increase the amount of ginger to one 2-inch piece. Omit the garlic and cornstarch. Add 1½ teaspoons chia seeds and 1 teaspoon sesame seeds and whisk to combine. Do not cook. Stored in an airtight container, the dressing will keep for 1 week in the refrigerator.

SIZZLING STIR-FRY SAUCE: Add 2 teaspoons ketchup and ½ teaspoon hot sauce.

SAVE FOR LATER

Stored in an airtight container, the stir-fry sauce will keep for 1 week in the refrigerator. Warm in a small saucepan over low heat before serving.

Dairy-Free Béchamel Sauce

Traditionally, béchamel sauce (aka white sauce) is thickened with a roux, which is made with equal amounts of flour and either butter or oil. In this fat-free adaptation, either cornstarch or arrowroot is used as a thickener to create a healthy version that's surprisingly as creamy and rich tasting as its high-fat cousin. Use this versatile sauce as a topping for cooked vegetables or pasta, or as a base for casseroles and stews.

MAKES 1 CUP, 4 SERVINGS

Per serving:

25 calories

0 g protein

1 g fat (0 g sat)

4 g carbs

148 mg sodium

110 mg calcium

0 g fiber

3½ teaspoons cornstarch or arrowroot

½ teaspoon garlic powder

½ teaspoon onion powder

1 cup plain nondairy milk

¼ teaspoon sea salt

⅛ teaspoon white pepper or freshly ground black pepper

⅛ teaspoon ground nutmeg

1. Put the cornstarch, garlic powder, and onion powder in a medium saucepan and whisk to combine.

2. Add the milk, salt, pepper, and nutmeg and cook over medium heat, whisking occasionally, until thickened, 2 to 3 minutes.

HERBED CREAM SAUCE: After the sauce has thickened, whisk in 1 tablespoon chopped fresh herbs, such as basil, dill, tarragon, or parsley.

NUTRITIONAL YEAST CHEESE SAUCE: Replace the cornstarch with 3½ teaspoons tapioca starch. After the sauce has thickened, whisk in ¼ cup nutritional yeast flakes, ½ teaspoon Dijon mustard, and ¼ teaspoon sweet or smoked paprika.

SAVE FOR LATER

Stored in an airtight container, the béchamel sauce will keep for 1 week in the refrigerator or 2 months in the freezer. Warm in a small saucepan over low heat before serving.

Cashew Cheese Sauce

**MAKES 1 CUP,
4 SERVINGS**

Per serving:

157 calories

2 g protein

1 g fat (0 g sat)

31 g carbs

1 mg sodium

10 mg calcium

2 g fiber

Soaked cashews are blended with vegetable broth and seasonings to create this luscious vegan cheese sauce. Spoon it warm over baked potatoes, cooked veggies, pasta, or casseroles. Alternatively, serve it chilled as a dip for crudités, tortilla chips, or pita bread.

¾   cup raw cashews, soaked in water for 2 hours and drained

½   cup low-sodium vegetable broth or water

⅓   cup nutritional yeast flakes

2   large cloves garlic

Juice of ½ lemon (2 tablespoons)

¼   teaspoon sea salt

⅛   teaspoon sweet paprika

1. Put all the ingredients in a blender and process until smooth. Scrape down the blender jar and process for 15 seconds longer.

2. Serve warm, cold, or at room temperature. For a warm sauce, transfer to a small saucepan and cook over medium heat, stirring constantly, just until heated through, 1 to 2 minutes.

NACHO CHEESE SAUCE: Add ½ orange, red, or yellow bell pepper, diced, and ½ teaspoon chili powder.

SAVE FOR LATER

Stored in an airtight container, the cheese sauce will keep for 1 week in the refrigerator or 2 months in the freezer.

Savory Onion Gravy

Sautéed onion and garlic along with nutritional yeast and poultry seasoning (yes, it's vegan) are used to achieve the savory flavor of this gluten-free gravy. Use the gravy as a topping for baked tofu or tempeh, baked or mashed potatoes, or other cooked vegetables or whole grains.

¼   cup finely diced yellow onion

1½ teaspoons olive oil

2   large cloves garlic, minced

1   cup low-sodium vegetable broth

2   tablespoons nutritional yeast flakes

1½ teaspoons reduced-sodium tamari

½   teaspoon poultry seasoning, or ¼ teaspoon ground sage
     and ¼ teaspoon dried thyme

¼   teaspoon sea salt

⅛   teaspoon freshly ground black pepper

¼   cup plain nondairy milk

2   tablespoons chickpea flour or other flour

1. Put the onion and oil in a medium saucepan and cook over medium heat, stirring occasionally, for 3 minutes. Add the garlic and cook, stirring occasionally, until the onion is soft, 1 to 2 minutes.

2. Add the broth, nutritional yeast, tamari, poultry seasoning, salt, and pepper and stir to combine. Bring to a boil over high heat. Cover, decrease the heat to low, and simmer for 3 minutes.

3. Put the milk and flour in a small bowl and whisk to combine. Add to the onion mixture and cook, whisking occasionally, until thickened, about 1 minute. Serve hot.

MUSHROOM GRAVY: When cooking the onion in the oil, add 1 cup coarsely chopped button or crimini mushrooms.

TIP: For even more flavor, add 1 tablespoon white wine or sherry when adding the broth.

MAKES 1¼ CUPS, 5 SERVINGS

Per serving:

47 calories

3 g protein

2 g fat (0 g sat)

4 g carbs

286 mg sodium

10 mg calcium

1 g fiber

SAVE FOR LATER

Stored in an airtight container, the onion gravy will keep for 1 week in the refrigerator or 2 months in the freezer. Warm in a small saucepan over low heat before serving.

Dressings, Salads, and Slaws

CHAPTER

FIVE

Lemon-Herb Vinaigrette

Stone-ground mustard and fresh lemon zest and juice are used to achieve this tangy vinaigrette, which tastes delicious on salads as well as on steamed or grilled veggies.

Zest and juice of 1 lemon (1½ teaspoons zest and ¼ cup juice)

2   tablespoons water

1   tablespoon stone-ground or spicy brown mustard

1   tablespoon nutritional yeast flakes

1   tablespoon minced garlic

½   cup olive oil

2   tablespoons chopped fresh parsley

Sea salt

Freshly ground black pepper

**MAKES 1 CUP,
8 SERVINGS**

Per serving:

125 calories

0 g protein

14 g fat (2 g sat)

1 g carbs

1 mg sodium

0 mg calcium

0 g fiber

Note: Analysis doesn't include sea salt and freshly ground black pepper to taste.

1. Put the lemon zest and juice, water, mustard, nutritional yeast, and garlic in a small bowl and whisk to combine.

2. While whisking constantly, slowly drizzle in the oil until well combined. Whisk in the parsley. Season with salt and pepper to taste.

AGAVE-DIJON DRESSING: Replace the lemon zest and juice with ¼ cup red wine vinegar or cider vinegar. Replace the stone-ground mustard with 1 tablespoon Dijon mustard and add 1½ tablespoons agave nectar.

HERBED BALSAMIC VINAIGRETTE: Replace the lemon zest and juice with ¼ cup balsamic vinegar. Replace the stone-ground mustard with 1 tablespoon Dijon mustard. Replace the fresh parsley with 1 teaspoon Italian seasoning.

SAVE FOR LATER

Stored in an airtight container, the vinaigrette will keep for 1 week in the refrigerator.

Creamy Ranch Dressing

**MAKES 1 CUP,
5 SERVINGS**

Per serving:

236 calories

13 g protein

2 g fat (0 g sat)

47 g carbs

61 mg sodium

130 mg calcium

7 g fiber

Chia seeds are amazing! These itty-bitty seeds can thicken all types of liquids, such as the soy milk used in this ranch dressing, which is rich and creamy without any added oil.

1	cup plain soy milk or other nondairy milk
2	tablespoons chopped fresh parsley
1½	tablespoons nutritional yeast flakes
1½	tablespoons cider vinegar
2	teaspoons chia seeds
¾	teaspoon dried dill weed
¾	teaspoon dried thyme
¾	teaspoon garlic powder
¾	teaspoon onion powder
¼	teaspoon freshly ground black pepper

1. Put all the ingredients in a blender and process until smooth. Scrape down the blender jar and let rest for 10 minutes.

2. Process the dressing again for 15 seconds to break up any clumps of chia seeds.

3. Transfer to an airtight container and refrigerate for 30 minutes to allow the dressing to thicken.

CREAMY ITALIAN VINAIGRETTE: Replace the cider vinegar with 2 tablespoons red wine vinegar. Replace the dill weed, thyme, garlic powder, and onion powder with 2 teaspoons Italian seasoning, 2 large cloves garlic, and ½ teaspoon crushed red pepper flakes.

SAVE FOR LATER

Stored in an airtight container, the dressing will keep for 1 week in the refrigerator.

Garlic-Tahini Dressing

Tahini, which is a paste made from ground sesame seeds, gives this garlicky dressing a velvety texture. Pour it over cooked grains, noodles, or vegetables, in addition to salads.

MAKES 1 CUP, 5 SERVINGS

Per serving:

125 calories

3 g protein

12 g fat (1 g sat)

2 g carbs

98 mg sodium

20 mg calcium

2 g fiber

½   cup water

¼   cup tahini

2   tablespoons flaxseed oil or hemp oil

2   tablespoons cider vinegar or lemon juice

1½ tablespoons minced garlic

1   tablespoon reduced-sodium tamari

¼   teaspoon freshly ground black pepper

1. Put all the ingredients in a blender and process until smooth.

2. Scrape down the blender jar and process for 15 seconds longer.

CURRY-CILANTRO DRESSING: Replace the flaxseed oil with 2 tablespoons olive oil. Add 2 tablespoons chopped fresh cilantro, 1 teaspoon curry powder, and ½ teaspoon ground cumin.

SAVE FOR LATER

Stored in an airtight container, the dressing will keep for 1 week in the refrigerator.

Berry and Melon Salad with Agave-Lime Dressing

MAKES 2 SERVINGS

Per serving:

96 calories

2 g protein

1 g fat (0 g sat)

23 g carbs

11 mg sodium

40 mg calcium

8 g fiber

A mix of colorful fresh berries and melon pieces are tossed with a mint-infused dressing made with agave nectar and lime juice. This light, refreshing salad is the perfect summertime treat.

2 tablespoons chopped fresh mint

Juice of ½ lime (1 tablespoon)

1 tablespoon agave nectar

1 cup cubed melon (such as cantaloupe, honeydew, or watermelon)

1 cup hulled and thinly sliced fresh strawberries

½ cup fresh blueberries or blackberries

½ cup fresh raspberries

1. Put the mint, lime juice, and agave nectar in a large bowl and whisk to combine.

2. Add the melon, strawberries, blueberries, and raspberries and gently stir to combine.

VARIATION: Replace the strawberries with 1 cup green or red seedless grapes, cut in half.

SAVE FOR LATER

Stored in an airtight container, the extra salad will keep for 2 days in the refrigerator.

Waldorf Salad with Yogurt Dressing

Crisp apples and celery, chewy dried fruit, and crunchy nuts are combined with a sweet yogurt dressing instead of a mayonnaise-based one in this healthier take on Waldorf salad. Serve it in a bowl or on a plate, straight up or on a bed of lettuce.

1	container (6 ounces) **plain or vanilla vegan yogurt**
1	tablespoon maple syrup
1	teaspoon lemon juice
2	large Fuji or Gala apples, cut into ½-inch cubes
½	cup thinly sliced celery
⅓	cup coarsely chopped pecans or walnuts
¼	cup raisins or dried cranberries
2	tablespoons chopped fresh parsley

1. To make the dressing, put the yogurt, maple syrup, and lemon juice in a small bowl and stir to combine.

2. To make the salad, put the apples, celery, pecans, raisins, and parsley in a medium bowl and stir to combine. Add the dressing and stir gently until evenly distributed. Serve immediately.

MAKES 2 SERVINGS

Per serving:

366 calories

4 g protein

17 g fat (1 g sat)

57 g carbs

26 mg sodium

300 mg calcium

9 g fiber

SAVE FOR LATER

Stored in an airtight container, the extra salad will keep for 2 days in the refrigerator.

Italian Pasta Salad

MAKES 3 SERVINGS

Per serving:

310 calories

7 g protein

15 g fat (2 g sat)

42 g carbs

19 mg sodium

20 mg calcium

2 g fiber

This filling salad is made with a colorful blend of fresh vegetables and cooked pasta, which are tossed together in a tangy balsamic vinaigrette. This recipe is readily adaptable, so feel free to replace any of the suggested vegetables with those lingering in your fridge. Serve it as is or on a bed of mixed greens or shredded lettuce.

5	ounces small pasta (such as bow ties, orzo, penne, or rotini)

Pinch sea salt (optional)

½	cup small broccoli florets
⅓	cup diced red or orange bell pepper
⅓	cup diced carrot
⅓	cup diced zucchini or yellow squash
1	green onion, thinly sliced
2	tablespoons chopped fresh basil or parsley
½	cup Herbed Balsamic Vinaigrette (page 47)

1. To cook the pasta, fill a large saucepan two-thirds full with water. Add the optional salt and bring to a boil over medium-high heat.

2. Add the pasta and cook, stirring occasionally, according to the package instructions or until tender. Drain the pasta in a colander, rinse it under cold water, and drain again. Transfer to a large bowl.

3. Add the broccoli, bell pepper, carrot, zucchini, green onion, and basil and stir to combine. Add the vinaigrette and gently toss until evenly distributed.

4. Serve immediately or cover and refrigerate for 30 minutes or longer to allow the flavors to blend.

SAVE FOR LATER

Stored in an airtight container, the pasta salad will keep for 5 days in the refrigerator.

Creamy Ranch-Dressed Potato Salad

All home cooks need a good potato salad in their repertoire, and this one couldn't be easier. For maximum flavor with minimal effort, homemade ranch dressing instead of vegan mayonnaise is used to harmonize the blend of cooked potatoes, celery, onion, and green onion.

MAKES 2 SERVINGS

Per serving:

221 calories

11 g protein

1 g fat (0 g sat)

44 g carbs

55 mg sodium

102 mg calcium

6 g fiber

Note: Analysis doesn't include sea salt and freshly ground black pepper to taste.

2   large red-skinned potatoes, cut into 1-inch cubes

2   stalks celery, thinly sliced

2   tablespoons diced red or yellow onion

1   green onion, thinly sliced

⅓   cup **Creamy Ranch Dressing** (page 48)

Sea salt

Freshly ground black pepper

1. Put the potatoes in a large saucepan and cover with water. Cook over medium-high heat until the potatoes are just tender and can be easily pierced with a knife, 10 to 15 minutes.

2. Drain the potatoes in a colander, rinse under cold water, and drain again. Transfer to a large bowl.

3. Add the celery, onion, and green onion and stir to combine. Add the dressing and gently stir until evenly distributed. Season with salt and pepper to taste.

4. Serve immediately or cover and refrigerate for 30 minutes or longer to allow the flavors to blend.

MARINATED POTATO SALAD: Replace the Creamy Ranch Dressing with ¼ cup Agave-Dijon Dressing (page 47), prepared with red wine vinegar.

SAVE FOR LATER

Stored in an airtight container, the potato salad will keep for 5 days in the refrigerator.

Kale Caesar Salad with Roasted Chickpea Croutons

MAKES 2 SERVINGS

Per serving:

312 calories

15 g protein

17 g fat (1 g sat)

30 g carbs

632 mg sodium

260 mg calcium

12 g fiber

For this updated version of Caesar salad, a garlicky tahini-based dressing is massaged into kale, which transforms the tough leaves into silky strips. But it's the final garnish of roasted chickpea croutons that truly elevates the flavor of this rustic salad.

ROASTED CHICKPEA CROUTONS

¾ cup cooked or canned chickpeas, drained and rinsed

1 teaspoon reduced-sodium tamari

1 teaspoon toasted sesame oil

1 teaspoon nutritional yeast flakes

½ teaspoon ground cumin

½ teaspoon garlic powder

¼ teaspoon chili powder

KALE SALAD

4 cups stemmed and very thinly sliced curly or Tuscan kale, lightly packed

2 teaspoons nutritional yeast flakes

6 tablespoons Garlic-Tahini Dressing (page 49)

1. To make the chickpea croutons, put the chickpeas on a clean kitchen towel or on paper towels and let air-dry for 10 minutes.

2. Preheat the oven to 425 degrees F. Line a baking sheet with parchment paper or a silicone baking mat.

3. Put the chickpeas in a small bowl. Add the tamari, oil, nutritional yeast, cumin, garlic powder, and chili powder and stir until well combined. Transfer to the lined baking sheet and spread the chickpeas into a single layer.

4. Bake for 25 to 30 minutes, or until the chickpeas are golden brown, dry, and slightly crunchy. Shake the pan every 10 minutes to ensure even baking,

5. To make the salad, put the kale in a large bowl and sprinkle with the nutritional yeast. Add the dressing and vigorously massage the kale with your hands until it begins to wilt and takes on a slightly cooked texture, 2 to 3 minutes. Season with salt and pepper to taste. Top with the chickpea croutons.

SAVE FOR LATER

Stored separately in individual airtight containers, the extra serving of kale and roasted chickpea croutons will keep for 3 days in the refrigerator.

TENDER GREENS CAESAR SALAD WITH ROASTED CHICKPEA CROUTONS: Replace the kale with 4 cups coarsely chopped romaine lettuce or baby spinach, lightly packed. Gently toss with the nutritional yeast and dressing. Do not massage the greens.

VARIATION: Replace the Garlic-Tahini Dressing with 3 tablespoons Curry-Cilantro Dressing (page 49) or 2 tablespoons Lemon-Herb Vinaigrette (page 47).

Taco Salad

MAKES 1 SERVING

Per serving:
290 calories
9 g protein
15 g fat (3 g sat)
33 g carbs
744 mg sodium
70 mg calcium
13 g fiber

When you're hungry for a salad that eats like a meal, taco salad fits the bill, as you get the irresistible flavor of tacos and a healthy salad all in one! If you have a head of lettuce and some chunky Avocado and Black Bean Salsa in the fridge, this can be assembled in mere minutes.

2   cups coarsely chopped romaine lettuce, lightly packed
½   cup Avocado and Black Bean Salsa (page 32), or ⅓ cup salsa
6   tortilla chips, crumbled
2   tablespoons shredded vegan Cheddar cheese

1. Put the lettuce and salsa in a medium bowl and toss gently. If desired, transfer to a large plate.

2. Top with the tortilla chips and shredded cheese. Serve immediately.

Veggie Chef's Salad

Typically a chef's salad is topped with meat, cheese, and hard-boiled eggs, but not this veggie-lover's version. Instead, a bed of mixed greens is topped with an assortment of fresh veggies, vegan cheese, and vegan bacon.

MAKES 1 SERVING

Per serving:

540 calories

28 g protein

10 g fat (1 g sat)

101 g carbs

799 mg sodium

260 mg calcium

14 g fiber

1¼ cups mixed baby greens or baby spinach, lightly packed

2 cherry tomatoes, halved, or ½ Roma tomato, diced

2 tablespoons thinly sliced red onion

4 thin slices cucumber

1 small carrot, shredded

2 radishes, thinly sliced

1 small gold or red beet, peeled and shredded

2 tablespoons shredded vegan Cheddar or mozzarella cheese

3 slices vegan bacon, cooked and cut into thin strips, or 2 tablespoons coconut bacon

¼ cup alfalfa sprouts or other sprouts

3 tablespoons Creamy Ranch Dressing (page 48) or Garlic-Tahini Dressing (page 49), or 2 tablespoons Lemon-Herb Vinaigrette or Herbed Balsamic Vinaigrette (page 47)

1. Put the baby greens in a large bowl or on a large platter.
2. Arrange the vegetables on top of the greens in this order: tomatoes, onion, cucumber, carrot, radishes, and beet.
3. Scatter the cheese, bacon, and sprouts over the vegetables.
4. Drizzle the dressing over the top. Serve immediately.

Tangy Coleslaw

MAKES 2 SERVINGS

Per serving:

204 calories

2 g protein

18 g fat (2 g sat)

13 g carbs

115 mg sodium

80 mg calcium

3 g fiber

Note: Analysis doesn't include sea salt and freshly ground black pepper to taste.

This quick and easy coleslaw is made with a combination of crunchy green and red cabbage and shredded carrot that's tossed with a tangy dressing. Serve this slaw as a side dish or as a crisp addition to sandwiches.

¾ cup shredded green cabbage, lightly packed

¾ cup shredded red cabbage, lightly packed

½ cup shredded carrot, lightly packed

1 green onion, thinly sliced

1½ tablespoons chopped fresh parsley

¼ cup Agave-Dijon Dressing (page 47), **prepared with cider vinegar**

½ teaspoon celery seeds (optional)

Sea salt

Freshly ground black pepper

1. Put the green cabbage, red cabbage, carrot, green onion, and parsley in a large bowl and toss to combine.

2. Put the dressing and optional celery seeds in a small bowl and stir to combine.

3. Pour the dressing over the vegetables and gently toss until evenly distributed. Season with salt and pepper to taste. Serve immediately or cover and refrigerate for 30 minutes or longer to allow the flavors to blend.

CLASSIC COLESLAW: Replace the Agave-Dijon Dressing with ¼ cup vegan mayonnaise or Creamy Ranch Dressing (page 48).

SAVE FOR LATER

Stored in an airtight container, the coleslaw will keep for 5 days in the refrigerator.

Sesame Slaw

A sweet-and-sour dressing unites a colorful blend of crisp and crunchy vegetables, leafy greens, mung bean sprouts, and edamame in this Asian-inspired slaw.

MAKES 2 SERVINGS

Per serving:

105 calories

4 g protein

4 g fat (0 g sat)

18 g carbs

290 mg sodium

120 mg calcium

6 g fiber

1   large leaf red curly kale, stemmed and cut into thin strips

1   large leaf rainbow or red Swiss chard, stem and leaf
    cut into thin strips

½   cup shredded savoy or green cabbage, lightly packed

½   cup shredded carrot, lightly packed

¼   cup diced red bell pepper

1   green onion, thinly sliced

2   tablespoons chopped fresh cilantro

¼   cup mung bean sprouts, lightly packed

2   tablespoons fresh or thawed frozen edamame

3   tablespoons Sesame-Ginger Dressing (page 42)

1. Put the kale, Swiss chard, cabbage, carrot, bell pepper, green onion, and cilantro in a large bowl and toss to combine. Scatter the sprouts and edamame over the top. Transfer to an airtight container and store for up to 3 days in the refrigerator.

2. For each serving, put half the slaw mixture in a medium bowl. Drizzle 1½ tablespoons of the dressing over the top and gently toss until evenly distributed. Serve immediately.

THAI PEANUT SLAW: Replace the edamame with 2 tablespoons coarsely chopped roasted peanuts and replace the Sesame-Ginger Dressing with 3 tablespoons Peanut Dressing (page 41).

SAVE FOR LATER

Stored separately in individual airtight containers, the extra serving of slaw and dressing will keep for 3 days in the refrigerator.

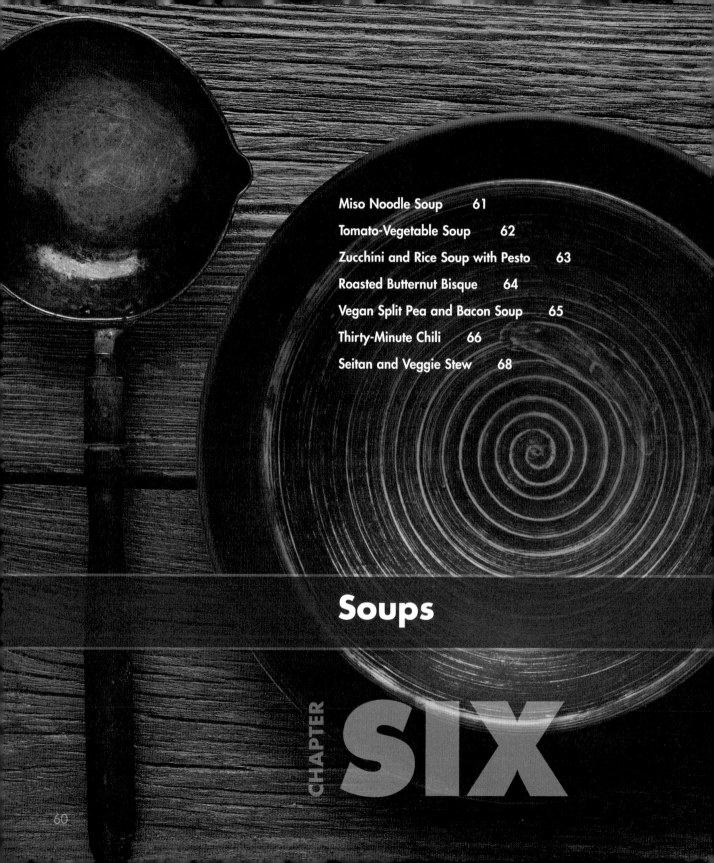

Soups

CHAPTER **SIX**

Miso Noodle Soup

Miso, traditionally made from fermented soybeans, is used to create the flavorful broth for this light yet filling soup, which contains buckwheat soba noodles, shiitake mushrooms, and bok choy. Any type of miso can be used for the soup, so select your favorite.

MAKES 2 SERVINGS

Per serving:

131 calories

5 g protein

5 g fat (1 g sat)

18 g carbs

705 mg sodium

80 mg calcium

3 g fiber

4   cups water

3   ounces buckwheat soba noodles or other noodles, broken in half

1   baby bok choy, cut into thin strips, or 2 cups baby spinach, lightly packed

⅔   cup thinly sliced shiitake or other mushrooms

¼   cup thinly sliced green onion

1   tablespoon peeled and grated fresh ginger

1½   tablespoons miso

1   teaspoon toasted sesame oil

1   teaspoon sesame seeds

1. Put the water, noodles, bok choy, mushrooms, green onion, and ginger in a large saucepan and stir to combine. Bring to a boil over high heat. Decrease the heat to low and simmer, stirring occasionally, until the noodles are tender, 7 to 10 minutes.

2. Put the miso in a small bowl. Add ½ cup of the hot broth from the saucepan and stir well to dissolve the miso.

3. Stir the miso mixture into the soup in the saucepan. Add the oil and sesame seeds and stir to combine. Serve hot.

VARIATION: Add ½ cup finely diced firm tofu to the finished soup.

SAVE FOR LATER

Stored in an airtight container, the extra serving of soup will keep for 3 days in the refrigerator. Warm in a small saucepan over medium-low heat before serving.

Tomato-Vegetable Soup

MAKES 2 SERVINGS

Per serving:

172 calories

8 g protein

35 g fat (0 g sat)

35 g carbs

610 mg sodium

150 mg calcium

9 g fiber

Note: Analysis doesn't include sea salt and freshly ground black pepper to taste.

Frozen mixed vegetables are convenient to keep on hand, as they can be used to quickly make a healthy side or main dish or to bulk up a soup like this one, which uses not only frozen vegetables but also a few fresh ones along with canned tomatoes.

1	can (14 ounces) **crushed tomatoes or diced tomatoes**
1	cup **low-sodium vegetable broth**
1	cup **coarsely chopped green cabbage, lightly packed**
¾	cup **frozen mixed vegetables** (carrots, corn, green beans, and peas)
1	small **turnip or potato, peeled and cut into ½-inch cubes**
½	cup **diced celery**
½	cup **diced red or yellow onion**
1	**bay leaf**
1½	teaspoons **Italian seasoning**
2	tablespoons **chopped fresh parsley**
1½	teaspoons **nutritional yeast flakes**
	Sea salt
	Freshly ground black pepper

1. Put the tomatoes, broth, cabbage, mixed vegetables, turnip, celery, onion, bay leaf, and Italian seasoning in a medium saucepan and stir to combine. Bring to a boil over high heat. Cover, decrease the heat to low, and simmer, stirring occasionally, until the vegetables are tender, 25 to 30 minutes.

2. Remove and discard the bay leaf. Add the parsley and nutritional yeast and stir until well incorporated. Season with salt and pepper to taste. Serve hot.

TOMATO-VEGETABLE SOUP WITH BARLEY: Add an additional ½ cup of vegetable broth and 3 tablespoons hulled or pearled barley, rinsed.

SAVE FOR LATER

Stored in an airtight container, the extra serving of soup will keep for 3 days in the refrigerator or 2 months in the freezer. Warm in a small saucepan over medium heat before serving.

Zucchini and Rice Soup with Pesto

Although this Italian-inspired soup contains only a handful of ingredients, it's quite flavorful, thanks to the fragrant pesto that's added at the end.

MAKES 2 SERVINGS

Per serving:

74 calories

4 g protein

4 g fat (2 g sat)

17 g carbs

201 mg sodium

20 mg calcium

4 g fiber

Note: Analysis doesn't include sea salt and freshly ground black pepper to taste.

¾ cup diced yellow onion

1½ teaspoons olive oil

¼ cup long-grain brown rice, rinsed

1 tablespoon minced garlic

2 cups low-sodium vegetable broth

1 large zucchini, cut in half lengthwise and thinly sliced

2 tablespoons Pesto or Sun-Dried Tomato-Basil Pesto (page 40)

2 teaspoons nutritional yeast flakes

½ teaspoon crushed red pepper flakes (optional)

Sea salt

Freshly ground black pepper

1. Put the onion and oil in a medium saucepan and cook over medium heat, stirring frequently, for 3 minutes. Add the rice and garlic and cook, stirring occasionally, for 1 minute.

2. Add the broth and stir to combine. Bring to a boil over high heat. Cover, decrease the heat to low, and simmer for 25 minutes.

3. Add the zucchini and simmer, stirring occasionally, until the rice is tender, 10 to 15 minutes.

4. Add the pesto, nutritional yeast, and optional red pepper flakes and stir until well incorporated. Season with salt and pepper to taste. Serve hot.

ZUCCHINI AND PASTA SOUP WITH PESTO: Omit the rice. When adding the zucchini, also add ¼ cup orzo, ditalini, or other small pasta.

SAVE FOR LATER

Stored in an airtight container, the extra serving of soup will keep for 3 days in the refrigerator. Warm in a small saucepan over medium heat before serving.

Roasted Butternut Bisque

MAKES 3 SERVINGS

Per serving:

254 calories

6 g protein

1 g fat (0 g sat)

62 g carbs

105 mg sodium

390 mg calcium

10 g fiber

Note: Analysis doesn't include sea salt and freshly ground black pepper to taste.

Oven roasting rather than sautéing or steaming will intensify the naturally sweet flavor of the butternut squash used in this soup. The squash is then blended with celery, shallot, ginger, and nondairy milk until velvety smooth.

1	butternut squash (1 to 1½ pounds), **halved lengthwise and seeded**
¾	cup low-sodium vegetable broth or water
1	stalk celery, diced
1	shallot, diced, or ½ cup diced yellow onion
2	teaspoons peeled and grated fresh ginger
1	cup plain nondairy milk

Sea salt

Freshly ground black pepper

1. Preheat the oven to 400 degrees F. Line a baking sheet with parchment paper or a silicone baking mat.

2. Put the butternut squash halves cut-side up on the lined baking sheet. Bake for 40 to 45 minutes, or until the squash is fork-tender. Remove from the oven. Let cool for 10 minutes.

3. While the squash is roasting, put the broth, celery, shallot, and ginger in a large saucepan. Bring to a boil over high heat. Decrease the heat to low and simmer, stirring occasionally, until the vegetables are tender, about 10 minutes. Remove from the heat.

4. With a spoon, scoop half the butternut squash flesh into a blender or food processor. Add the celery mixture and process until smooth. Transfer the blended mixture to the saucepan.

5. Using a spoon, scoop the flesh of the remaining butternut squash into the blender or food processor. Add the milk and process until smooth. Add to the soup in the saucepan and stir to combine. Season with salt and pepper to taste. Serve hot.

APPLE-BUTTERNUT BISQUE: To the simmering celery mixture, add 1 apple, peeled, cored, and diced, and ½ teaspoon ground cinnamon.

VARIATION: Replace the butternut squash with 1 to 1½ pounds of other winter squash, such as acorn, buttercup, or turban.

SAVE FOR LATER

Stored in an airtight container, the extra servings of soup will keep for 3 days in the refrigerator. Warm in a small saucepan over medium heat before serving.

Vegan Split Pea and Bacon Soup

Fall and winter are ideal for making split pea soup. For this thick and filling version, dried split peas are simmered with aromatic vegetables, then bits of vegan bacon are added to impart a rich, smoky flavor.

4	cups water
1	cup dried split peas, sorted and rinsed
1	small yellow onion, diced
2	carrots, cut in half lengthwise and thinly sliced
2	stalks celery, cut in half lengthwise and thinly sliced
1	tablespoon minced garlic
1	bay leaf
½	teaspoon dried basil
½	teaspoon dried oregano
½	teaspoon dried thyme
½	teaspoon chili powder
4	slices vegan bacon, cooked and coarsely chopped
¼	cup chopped fresh parsley, lightly packed
1	tablespoon nutritional yeast flakes
	Sea salt
	Freshly ground black pepper

MAKES 3 SERVINGS

Per serving:

207 calories

19 g protein

2 g fat (0 g sat)

42 g carbs

275 mg sodium

40 mg calcium

17 g fiber

Note: Analysis doesn't include sea salt and freshly ground black pepper to taste.

1. Put the water, split peas, onion, carrots, celery, garlic, bay leaf, basil, oregano, thyme, and chili powder in a large saucepan and stir to combine. Bring to a boil over high heat. Cover, decrease the heat to low, and simmer, stirring occasionally, until the peas are tender, about 1 hour.

2. Remove and discard the bay leaf. Add the bacon, parsley, and nutritional yeast and stir until well incorporated. Season with salt and pepper to taste. Serve hot.

VEGETARIAN NAVY BEAN AND BACON SOUP: Replace the split peas with 1 cup dried navy beans, sorted and rinsed, and cook for an additional 30 minutes, or until the beans are tender.

SAVE FOR LATER

Stored in an airtight container, the extra servings of soup will keep for 3 days in the refrigerator or 2 months in the freezer. Warm in a small saucepan over medium heat before serving.

Thirty-Minute Chili

MAKES 4 SERVINGS

Per serving:

204 calories

9 g protein

4 g fat (1 g sat)

34 g carbs

708 mg sodium

110 mg calcium

12 g fiber

*Note: Analysis doesn't include
sea salt and freshly ground black
pepper to taste.*

This hearty chili is packed with flavor, thanks to the ample amount of spices. Because it uses canned tomatoes and beans, it can be on the table in less than thirty minutes!

1	cup diced red or yellow onion
1	red bell pepper, diced
1	serrano or jalapeño chile, seeded and finely diced
1	tablespoon olive oil
1	tablespoon minced garlic
1	tablespoon chili powder
1	teaspoon ground cumin
1	teaspoon dried oregano
1	can (15 ounces) **mixed beans or black, pinto, or kidney beans, drained and rinsed**
1	can (14 ounces) **crushed tomatoes**
1	can (14 ounces) **fire-roasted or regular diced tomatoes**
¼	cup chopped fresh cilantro or parsley, lightly packed

Juice of 1 lime (2 tablespoons)

Sea salt

Freshly ground black pepper

1. Put the onion, bell pepper, chile, and oil in a large saucepan and cook over medium heat, stirring occasionally, for 5 minutes. Add the garlic, chili powder, cumin, and oregano and cook, stirring occasionally, for 1 minute.

2. Add the beans, crushed tomatoes, and diced tomatoes and stir to combine. Cover, decrease the heat to low, and simmer until the vegetables are tender, about 15 minutes.

3. Add the cilantro and lime juice and stir until well incorporated. Season with salt and pepper to taste. Serve hot.

SAVE FOR LATER

Stored in an airtight container, the extra servings of chili will keep for 3 days in the refrigerator or 2 months in the freezer. Warm in a small saucepan over medium heat before serving.

Seitan and Veggie Stew

MAKES 4 SERVINGS

Per serving:

181 calories

19 g protein

1 g fat (0 g sat)

19 g carbs

363 mg sodium

20 mg calcium

4 g fiber

Depending on how it's prepared and seasoned, seitan is great for mimicking the flavor and texture of meat. For this recipe, chewy pieces of seitan and vegetables are simmered with vegetable broth, red wine, and a few condiments from the fridge to create this meatless version of beef stew.

3	cups low-sodium vegetable broth
1	potato, small turnip, or parsnip, peeled and cut into 1-inch cubes
1	package (10 ounces) frozen peas and carrots
1	package (8 ounces) seitan, cut into bite-sized cubes or strips
1	cup thinly sliced button or crimini mushrooms
2	stalks celery, sliced
1	small yellow onion, cut into 1-inch pieces
¼	cup red wine
1	tablespoon tomato paste or ketchup
1	tablespoon reduced-sodium tamari
1½	teaspoons Italian seasoning
¼	teaspoon freshly ground black pepper
2	tablespoons chickpea flour or other flour
2	tablespoons water
¼	cup chopped fresh parsley, lightly packed

1. Put the broth, potato, peas and carrots, seitan, mushrooms, celery, onion, wine, tomato paste, tamari, Italian seasoning, and pepper in a large saucepan and stir to combine. Bring to a boil over high heat. Cover, decrease the heat to low, and simmer, stirring occasionally, until the vegetables are tender, about 20 minutes.

2. Put the flour and water in a small bowl and stir to combine. Add the flour mixture to the stew in the saucepan and cook, stirring occasionally, until thickened, 2 to 3 minutes. Add the parsley and stir until well incorporated. Serve hot.

SAVE FOR LATER

Stored in an airtight container, the extra servings of stew will keep for 3 days in the refrigerator or 2 months in the freezer. Warm in a small saucepan over medium heat before serving.

Wraps and Sandwiches

CHAPTER SEVEN

Tofu and Slaw Spring Rolls

**MAKES 4 SPRING ROLLS,
2 SERVINGS**

Per serving:

380 calories

19 g protein

15 g fat (2 g sat)

43 g carbs

493 mg sodium

140 mg calcium

9 g fiber

Packaged rice paper can be found in the international section of most grocery stores, and because it's dried, rice paper can be stored in a cabinet or the pantry until needed. For these tasty spring rolls, rice paper encases a colorful veggie slaw and strips of smoked tofu. The rolls are then served with a flavorful dipping sauce.

4   (8-inch or larger) **round rice papers**

1   **serving Sesame Slaw or Thai Peanut Slaw** (page 59)

1   **package** (6 ounces) **smoked or baked tofu, cut lengthwise into 8 strips**

¼   cup **Sesame-Ginger Dressing** (page 42) **or Spicy Peanut Sauce** (page 41)

1. Fill a 9-inch round pie pan with warm water. Working with 1 rice paper at a time, submerge it in the water and soak it until soft and pliable, 10 to 20 seconds. Shake off the excess water and put the rice paper on a large plate or cutting board.

2. To assemble each spring roll, put one-quarter of the slaw mixture about 1 inch from the bottom and sides of the rice paper. Put two strips of the smoked tofu on top of the slaw.

3. To roll each spring roll, fold the bottom half of the rice paper over the filling, fold in each side toward the center over the filling, and roll up from the bottom edge to enclose the filling. Put the spring roll seam-side down in an airtight container.

4. Repeat the assembly and rolling procedure with the remaining rice papers, slaw, and tofu. Serve with the dressing on the side as a dipping sauce.

SAVE FOR LATER

Stored in an airtight container, the extra spring rolls will keep for 2 days in the refrigerator.

Hummus and Veggie Wrap

Wraps taste best when they're freshly made because they can quickly become soggy, especially when they're made with moist veggies. That's why this recipe makes only one wrap. But you can quickly roll one up on the fly, since all the ingredients can be prepared in advance and stored in separate containers in the fridge for several days.

1   (8-inch or larger) **flour tortilla**

1   **large lettuce leaf** (such as Boston or looseleaf), ½ **cup baby lettuce or spinach**, or ½ **cup shredded raw vegetables**

⅓   cup **Hummus, Curry-Cilantro Hummus, Olive Hummus, or Roasted Red Pepper Hummus** (page 34)

4   slices cucumber

2   slices tomato

¼   cup alfalfa sprouts or other sprouts

1. For easier rolling, warm the tortilla in a large nonstick skillet over medium heat, 1 minute per side. Alternatively, microwave the tortilla for 20 to 30 seconds.

2. To assemble the wrap, put the tortilla on a large plate. Put the lettuce leaf horizontally in the center of the tortilla. Spread the hummus on top of the lettuce. Layer the cucumber, tomato, and sprouts on top of the hummus.

3. To roll the wrap, fold the bottom half of the tortilla over the filling, fold in each side toward the center over the filling, and roll up from the bottom edge to enclose the filling. Serve immediately.

BABA AND VEGGIE WRAP: Replace the hummus with ⅓ cup Baba Ganoush (page 35).

MAKES 1 WRAP, 1 SERVING

Per serving:

310 calories

12 g protein

12 g fat (2 g sat)

44 g carbs

778 mg sodium

120 mg calcium

7 g fiber

TO-GO TIP

Put the wrap seam-side down in an airtight container.

Loaded Bean Burritos

**MAKES 2 BURRITOS,
2 SERVINGS**

Per serving:

312 calories

12 g protein

7 g fat (2 g sat)

47 g carbs

715 mg sodium

80 mg calcium

9 g fiber

These flavor-packed burritos are filled with a mixture of vegetarian refried beans, salsa, vegan cheese, guacamole, and crisp lettuce.

2	(8-inch or larger) **flour tortillas**
⅔	cup **vegetarian refried beans,** warmed
¼	cup Black Bean and Corn Salsa (page 32) **or salsa**
¼	cup **shredded vegan Cheddar cheese**
¼	cup Zesty Guacamole (page 33), **or ½ avocado, mashed or diced**
2	**large lettuce leaves** (such as romaine or looseleaf), **shredded**

1. For easier rolling, warm the tortillas in a large nonstick skillet over medium heat, 1 minute per side. Alternatively, microwave the tortillas for for 20 to 30 seconds.

2. To assemble each burrito, put the tortilla on a large plate. Spread ⅓ cup of the refried beans horizontally in the center of the tortilla. Top with 2 tablespoons of the salsa, 2 tablespoons of the cheese, 2 tablespoons of the guacamole, and half the shredded lettuce.

3. To roll the burrito, fold the bottom half of the tortilla over the filling, fold in each side toward the center over the filling, and roll up from the bottom edge to enclose the filling. Repeat the assembly and rolling procedure with the remaining tortilla, refried beans, salsa, cheese, guacamole, and lettuce.

RICE AND BEAN BURRITOS: Replace the refried beans and salsa with 1 cup Spanish Rice with Corn and Beans (page 95), and use ½ cup of the mixture for each burrito.

SAVE FOR LATER

Stored seam-side down in an airtight container, the extra burrito will keep for 2 days in the refrigerator.

TO-GO TIP

Put the burrito seam-side down in an airtight container.

Mexicali Corn Quesadillas

Beans, corn, and shredded vegan cheese are mashed with flavorful seasonings to make the filling for these tasty quesadillas. Enjoy them for lunch, dinner, or a snack, topped with salsa, vegan sour cream, and guacamole or diced avocado.

¾ cup cooked beans (such as black, kidney, or pinto)

⅓ cup canned corn, drained and rinsed, or ⅓ cup frozen corn kernels, thawed

⅓ cup shredded vegan cheese

2 tablespoons finely diced red or yellow onion

2 tablespoons salsa, plus additional for garnish

1½ tablespoons nutritional yeast flakes

1 teaspoon chili powder

2 (8-inch or larger) flour tortillas

¼ cup Zesty Guacamole (page 33), or ½ avocado, mashed or diced

2 tablespoons vegan sour cream

1. To make the filling, put the beans, corn, cheese, onion, salsa, nutritional yeast, and chili powder in a medium bowl and coarsely mash with a fork or potato masher to combine.

2. To assemble the quesadillas, put the tortillas on a cutting board or work surface. Spoon half the filling mixture over half of each tortilla. Fold each tortilla over to enclose the filling.

3. Lightly oil a large nonstick skillet or mist it with cooking spray. Heat over medium heat.

4. Cook the quesadillas in the hot skillet until lightly browned on the bottom, 2 to 3 minutes. Flip over the quesadillas and cook until lightly browned on the other side, 2 to 3 minutes longer. Garnish each quesadilla with additional salsa and half the guacamole and sour cream.

MAKES 2 QUESADILLAS, 2 SERVINGS

Per serving:

445 calories

23 g protein

11 g fat (2 g sat)

62 g carbs

670 mg sodium

120 mg calcium

15 g fiber

SAVE FOR LATER

Stored in an airtight container, the extra quesadilla will keep for 2 days in the refrigerator. Serve cold or wrap in foil and warm at 350 degrees F in the oven or a toaster oven until heated through, about 10 minutes.

Seitan Street Tacos

**MAKES 4 TACOS,
2 SERVINGS**

Per serving:

702 calories

39 g protein

35 g fat (5 g sat)

64 g carbs

488 mg sodium

150 mg calcium

12 g fiber

These soft, meatless tacos are filled with seasoned seitan, then topped with shredded cheese and a cabbage slaw that's flavored with fresh cilantro. They're the perfect meal for Taco Tuesday or any day of the week. *Olé!*

1	package (8 ounces) **seitan**, coarsely chopped
½	cup finely diced **yellow onion**
1	tablespoon **olive oil** or other oil
2	large cloves **garlic**, minced
1	tablespoon **nutritional yeast flakes**
1	teaspoon **chili powder**
½	teaspoon **dried oregano**
½	teaspoon **ground cumin**
¼	teaspoon **hot sauce** or chipotle chile powder

Juice of 1 **lime** (2 tablespoons)

2	cups **Tangy Coleslaw** (page 58)
¼	cup chopped **fresh cilantro**, lightly packed
8	(6-inch) **corn tortillas**, or 4 (8-inch) **flour tortillas**
¼	cup shredded **vegan cheese**

1. To make the seitan filling, put the seitan, onion, and oil in a large nonstick skillet and cook over medium heat, stirring occasionally, for 5 minutes. Add the garlic, nutritional yeast, chili powder, oregano, cumin, and hot sauce and cook, stirring occasionally, until the seitan is lightly browned, 2 to 3 minutes. Add the lime juice and stir to combine.

2. Put the coleslaw and cilantro in a small bowl and stir to combine.

3. For easier handling, warm each tortilla in a large nonstick skillet over medium heat, 20 to 30 seconds per side. Alternatively, microwave the tortillas for 10 to 20 seconds.

4. To assemble each taco, stack two corn tortillas on top of each other. If using flour tortillas, use only one tortilla for each taco. Fill each taco with one-quarter of the seitan mixture and top with 1 tablespoon of the cheese and one-quarter of the coleslaw.

SAVE FOR LATER

Stored in separate airtight containers, the extra seitan filling and coleslaw will keep for 3 days in the refrigerator.

CRUNCHY SEITAN TACOS: Replace the tortillas with 4 taco shells, warmed for crispier and more flavorful shells. To warm, preheat the oven to 325 degrees F. Unwrap the shells, pull them apart slightly (but not completely) and put them on a baking sheet. Keeping them slightly stacked will prevent them from caving in and closing up. Put a wadded-up ball of parchment paper in the first taco in the stack to keep it open. Bake for 6 to 7 minutes, or until crisp. Fill each taco shell with one-quarter of the seitan mixture. Top each taco with 1 tablespoon shredded vegan cheese and your choice of toppings, such as shredded lettuce, diced tomatoes, and guacamole or diced avocado. Serve immediately.

No Yolks Egg Salad

**MAKES 1½ CUPS,
2 SERVINGS**

Per serving:

186 calories

13 g protein

12 g fat (2 g sat)

9 g carbs

747 mg sodium

240 mg calcium

2 g fiber

Tofu is a great replacement for eggs in recipes, including hard-boiled eggs, as with this veganized version of egg salad. Turmeric is the secret ingredient that gives this dish a traditional yellow hue. In addition to making an awesome sandwich filling, it's great as a salad on top of mixed greens or as a snack served with crackers.

8	ounces firm or extra-firm tofu
1	tablespoon nutritional yeast flakes
2	teaspoons lemon juice
½	teaspoon garlic powder
½	teaspoon onion powder
½	teaspoon sea salt
¼	teaspoon celery seeds (optional)
¼	teaspoon ground turmeric
⅛	teaspoon freshly ground black pepper
¼	cup vegan mayonnaise
1	stalk celery, finely diced
1	green onion, thinly sliced
2	tablespoons chopped fresh parsley
1	tablespoon pickle relish

1. Using your fingers, crumble the tofu into a medium bowl. Add the nutritional yeast, lemon juice, garlic powder, onion powder, salt, optional celery seeds, turmeric, and pepper. Using a potato masher or a fork, mash the tofu with the seasonings until well combined.

2. Add the mayonnaise, celery, green onion, parsley, and relish and stir to combine. Set aside for 10 minutes to allow the flavors to blend.

SAVE FOR LATER

Stored in an airtight container, the egg salad will keep for 5 days in the refrigerator.

Classic BLT

If you have vegan bacon on hand, you can quickly make this classic sandwich. To ramp up the flavor even more, top the toasted bread with spicy or whole-grain mustard instead of mayo.

2   slices whole-grain bread or other bread, toasted
2   tablespoons vegan mayonnaise or spicy or whole-grain mustard
1   large lettuce leaf (such as Boston or looseleaf)
4   slices vegan bacon, cooked
1   Roma tomato, cut into 4 slices

1. Put the toasted bread on a large plate or cutting board.
2. Spread 1 tablespoon of the mayonnaise over each slice.
3. Top one slice of bread with the lettuce, bacon, and tomato. Cover with the remaining slice of bread, spread-side down. Slice in half on the diagonal before serving.

MAKES 1 SERVING

Per serving:
308 calories
15 g protein
13 g fat (1 g sat)
31 g carbs
1103 mg sodium
250 mg calcium
3 g fiber

Versatile Veggie-Bean Burgers

MAKES 4 BURGERS

Per serving:

209 calories

11 g protein

2 g fat (0 g sat)

38 g carbs

574 mg sodium

110 mg calcium

12 g fiber

Get ready to express your culinary creativity! The type of beans and seasonings you choose will determine the final flavor of these plump veggie burgers. Using this basic recipe as your guide, you can make an endless array of tasty burgers to perfectly suit your palate. Serve them on buns with your favorite toppings and condiments.

3	tablespoons warm water
1	teaspoon chia seeds, or 1 tablespoon ground flaxseeds or flaxseed meal
1	cup old-fashioned rolled oats
1	carrot, cut into 4 pieces
1	stalk celery, cut into 4 pieces
½	small onion, cut into 4 pieces
1	jalapeño chile, seeded and finely diced (optional)
3	large cloves garlic
1	can (15 ounces) black beans, other beans, or lentils, drained and rinsed
¼	cup chopped fresh parsley or cilantro, lightly packed
2	tablespoons nutritional yeast flakes
2	teaspoons chili powder, or 1 teaspoon curry powder
1½	teaspoons dried basil, oregano, marjoram, thyme, or rosemary, or a combination
½	teaspoon ground cumin
½	teaspoon sea salt
¼	teaspoon freshly ground black pepper

1. Put the water and chia seeds in a small bowl and stir to combine. Let rest for 10 minutes, until the mixture thickens into a gel.

2. Put the oats, carrot, celery, onion, optional chile, and garlic in a food processor and process until coarsely chopped. Scrape down the work bowl. Add the chia seed mixture, beans, parsley, nutritional yeast, chili powder, basil, cumin, salt, and pepper and process until evenly distributed and the beans are coarsely chopped.

SAVE FOR LATER

Stored in an airtight container, the cooked burgers will keep for 3 days in the refrigerator or 3 months in the freezer. Warm the refrigerated burgers in a small skillet over medium-low heat, 2 minutes per side. Reheat the frozen burgers in a small skillet over medium heat until hot, 3 minutes per side.

3. Transfer to a medium bowl and refrigerate for 15 minutes. Using your hands, shape the mixture into four patties, and put the patties on a large plate. Flatten each patty into a 4-inch circle. Refrigerate for at least 1 hour to let the patties firm up slightly.

4. Lightly oil a large nonstick skillet or mist it with cooking spray. Heat over medium-high heat.

5. When the skillet is hot, cook the burgers until golden brown on both sides, 7 to 8 minutes per side. Add more oil to the skillet as needed to prevent sticking.

VARIATION: Replace the carrot with ½ cup peeled and coarsely chopped beet, potato, or sweet potato.

Portobello Mushroom Burgers

**MAKES 2 BURGERS,
2 SERVINGS**

Per serving:

115 calories

5 g protein

7 g fat (1 g sat)

11 g carbs

93 mg sodium

400 mg calcium

7 g fiber

Whole portobello mushrooms make great meatless burgers with very little effort. A simple marinade made with balsamic vinegar is rubbed on the mushroom caps, which are then cooked until tender in a skillet. Serve them on buns or rolls, topped with your favorite fixin's.

1	tablespoon balsamic vinegar
1	tablespoon olive oil
½	teaspoon dried basil
½	teaspoon dried oregano
½	teaspoon garlic powder
2	large portobello mushrooms

1. To make the marinade, put the vinegar, oil, basil, oregano, and garlic powder in a small bowl and whisk to combine.

2. Remove and discard the mushroom stems. Put the mushroom caps on a large plate. Using your fingers, rub the marinade over both sides of each mushroom. Set aside for 5 minutes to marinate.

3. Lightly oil a large nonstick skillet or mist it with cooking spray. Heat over medium-high heat.

4. When the skillet is hot, cook the mushrooms, gill-side up, for 5 minutes. Flip over the mushrooms and cook until tender, 2 to 3 minutes longer.

VARIATION: Replace the balsamic marinade with 2 tablespoons Herbed Balsamic Vinaigrette (page 47).

SAVE FOR LATER

Stored in an airtight container, the extra cooked mushroom will keep for 3 days in the refrigerator.

CHAPTER EIGHT

Side Dishes

Smoky-Bacon Brussels Sprouts

MAKES 2 SERVINGS

Per serving:

106 calories

6 g protein

5 g fat (1 g sat)

10 g carbs

265 mg sodium

40 mg calcium

4 g fiber

Note: Analysis doesn't include sea salt and freshly ground black pepper to taste.

Think you hate Brussels sprouts? Think again. You'll go from a hater to a lover after tasting these Brussels sprouts, which are first cooked in a bit of vegetable stock and then sautéed in toasted sesame oil with a shallot and vegan bacon.

2   cups fresh Brussels sprouts, cut in half lengthwise, or 1 package (10 ounces) frozen Brussels sprouts, thawed and cut in half lengthwise

¼   cup low-sodium vegetable broth

3   slices vegan bacon, cut into thin strips

1   small shallot, diced, or ¼ cup diced red onion

1½   teaspoons toasted sesame oil

½   teaspoon dried thyme

Sea salt

Freshly ground black pepper

1. Put the Brussels sprouts and vegetable broth in a large nonstick skillet. Cover and cook over medium-high heat for 5 minutes. Remove the lid and cook until all the broth has evaporated, 1 to 2 minutes.

2. Add the bacon, shallot, oil, and thyme and cook, stirring occasionally, until the Brussels sprouts and bacon are lightly browned, about 5 minutes. Season with salt and pepper to taste. Serve hot.

MAPLE-BACON BRUSSELS SPROUTS: Replace the toasted sesame oil with 1½ teaspoons olive oil. When the Brussels sprouts are lightly browned, add 1 tablespoon maple syrup and 1½ teaspoons balsamic vinegar or cider vinegar.

SAVE FOR LATER

Stored in an airtight container, the extra serving of Brussels sprouts will keep for 3 days in the refrigerator. Warm in a small saucepan or skillet over medium-low heat before serving.

Candied-Ginger Baby Carrots

These irresistible candied carrots are cooked with agave nectar, vegan butter, and a bit of water until the cooking liquid is reduced to a sweet glaze. For ease, whole baby carrots are used in this recipe, but if you prefer, you can use regular carrots that have been cut into comparable lengths.

1½ cups whole baby carrots or cut carrots in 2-inch pieces

¼ cup water

2 tablespoons agave nectar

2 teaspoons vegan butter or coconut oil

1 tablespoon peeled and grated fresh ginger (optional)

Sea salt

1. Put the carrots, water, agave nectar, butter, and optional ginger in a large saucepan and stir to combine. Cover and cook over medium heat for 8 minutes.

2. Remove the lid and cook, stirring occasionally, until the carrots are tender and the cooking liquid thickens to a glaze, 3 to 5 minutes. Season with salt to taste. Serve hot.

VARIATION: Replace the carrots with 1½ cups of other root vegetables, such as peeled beets, parsnips, rutabagas, turnips, or sweet potatoes, cut into 2-inch pieces.

MAKES 2 SERVINGS

Per serving:

123 calories

1 g protein

4 g fat (1 g sat)

23 g carbs

98 mg sodium

0 mg calcium

2 g fiber

Note: Analysis doesn't include sea salt and freshly ground black pepper to taste.

SAVE FOR LATER

Stored in an airtight container, the extra serving of carrots will keep for 3 days in the refrigerator. Warm in a small saucepan or skillet over medium-low heat before serving.

Coconut Creamed Corn

MAKES 2 SERVINGS

Per serving:

232 calories

7 g protein

4 g fat (1 g sat)

44 g carbs

67 mg sodium

160 mg calcium

3 g fiber

Note: Analysis doesn't include sea salt and freshly ground black pepper to taste.

The naturally sweet flavor of corn is elevated to new heights when it's simmered with coconut milk, green onion, and thyme. You'll never buy canned creamed corn again, as the flavor of this rich, velvety version blows it away!

1	package (10 ounces) **frozen corn kernels**
⅔	cup plain **coconut milk beverage**
1	**green onion**, thinly sliced
1	tablespoon **nutritional yeast flakes**
1	teaspoon **dried thyme**
1	teaspoon **vegan butter**
1	tablespoon **water**
1½	teaspoons **arrowroot** or **cornstarch**
	Sea salt
	Freshly ground black pepper

1. Put the corn, milk, green onion, nutritional yeast, thyme, and butter in a medium saucepan and stir to combine. Cover and cook over medium heat for 8 minutes. Remove the lid.

2. Put the water and arrowroot in a small bowl and stir to combine. Add to the corn mixture and cook, stirring occasionally, until slightly thickened, 1 to 2 minutes. Season with salt and pepper to taste. Serve hot.

SAVE FOR LATER

Stored in an airtight container, the extra serving of creamed corn will keep for 3 days in the refrigerator. Warm in a small saucepan over medium-low heat before serving.

Garlicky Greens

There are so many types of leafy greens. Each one has a different flavor and texture, and they're all so good for you! You can't go wrong when you cook up a batch of leafy greens with onion and garlic. Any variety of leafy greens can be used for this recipe.

½   cup diced yellow onion

2   teaspoons olive oil

1   bunch (1 pound) **collard greens or other leafy greens**
(such as kale, mustard greens, spinach, Swiss chard, or turnip greens), stemmed and thinly sliced

1½ tablespoons minced garlic

1   tablespoon nutritional yeast flakes

Sea salt

Freshly ground black pepper

Crushed red pepper flakes or hot sauce (optional)

1. Put the onion and oil in a large nonstick skillet and cook over medium heat, stirring occasionally, for 5 minutes.

2. Add the leafy greens and garlic and cook, stirring occasionally, until the greens are tender, 5 to 7 minutes.

3. Add the nutritional yeast and stir until well incorporated. Season with salt, pepper, and optional red pepper flakes to taste. Serve hot.

GARLICKY GREENS AND BEANS: Add 1 can (15 ounces) beans (such as chickpeas or navy, kidney, or pinto beans), drained and rinsed.

MAKES 2 SERVINGS

Per serving:

172 calories

8 g protein

8 g fat (1 g sat)

22 g carbs

7 mg sodium

360 mg calcium

8 g fiber

Note: Analysis doesn't include sea salt and freshly ground black pepper to taste.

SAVE FOR LATER

Stored in an airtight container, the extra serving of greens will keep for 3 days in the refrigerator. Warm in a small saucepan over medium-low heat before serving.

Caribbean Black Beans with Mango Salsa

MAKES 2 SERVINGS

Per serving:

300 calories

14 g protein

6 g fat (4 g sat)

62 g carbs

628 mg sodium

100 mg calcium

18 g fiber

Note: Analysis doesn't include sea salt and freshly ground black pepper to taste.

This recipe gets its inspiration from the Caribbean Islands. Black beans are flavored with jalapeño chile, citrus juice, ginger, and allspice and then topped with a sweet mango salsa. For an authentic island meal, serve the beans alongside cooked rice, although they're equally tasty served with tortilla or plantain chips.

MANGO SALSA

½ mango, peeled and diced

¼ cup diced red bell pepper

¼ cup diced red onion

2 tablespoons chopped fresh cilantro

1½ teaspoons lime juice

Sea salt

Freshly ground black pepper

CARIBBEAN BLACK BEANS

½ cup diced red or yellow onion

1 jalapeño chile, seeded and finely diced

2 teaspoons coconut oil

1 tablespoon peeled and grated fresh ginger

½ teaspoon dried thyme

¼ teaspoon ground allspice

1 can (15 ounces) black beans, drained and rinsed

¼ cup orange juice, or juice of 1 lime (2 tablespoons)

Sea salt

Freshly ground black pepper

1. To make the mango salsa, put the first five ingredients in a medium bowl and stir to combine. Season with salt and pepper to taste.

2. To make the black beans, put the onion, chile, and oil in small saucepan and cook over medium heat, stirring occasionally, for 3 minutes. Add the ginger, thyme, and allspice and cook, stirring occasionally, for 1 minute.

3. Add the black beans and orange juice and stir to combine. Decrease the heat to low and cook, stirring occasionally, for 3 minutes.

4. Using a spoon, fork, or potato masher, mash one-quarter of the black beans against the side of the saucepan and continue to cook until the mixture is slightly thickened, 1 to 2 minutes. Season with salt and pepper to taste. Top each serving with half the mango salsa. Serve hot.

SAVE FOR LATER

Stored separately in airtight containers, the extra serving of black beans and mango salsa will keep for 3 days in the refrigerator. Warm the beans in a small saucepan over medium-low heat before serving.

Sesame Green Beans and Bell Pepper

Green beans and red bell pepper are stir-fried in toasted sesame oil along with fresh ginger and garlic until they're crisp-tender, then they're topped with sesame seeds.

8   ounces fresh green beans, cut in half, or 1 package (10 ounces) **frozen cut green beans**

1   red or orange bell pepper, cut into 2-inch strips

1½ tablespoons minced garlic

1½ tablespoons peeled and grated fresh ginger

1½ teaspoons toasted sesame oil

1   tablespoon sesame seeds

½   teaspoon crushed red pepper flakes

¼   teaspoon freshly ground black pepper

¼   cup chopped fresh parsley, lightly packed

2   teaspoons reduced-sodium tamari

1. Put the green beans, bell pepper, garlic, ginger, and oil in a large non-stick skillet and cook over medium-high heat, stirring occasionally, for 5 minutes.
2. Add the sesame seeds, red pepper flakes, and pepper and cook, stirring occasionally, until the green beans are crisp-tender, 1 to 2 minutes.
3. Add the parsley and tamari and stir until well incorporated. Serve hot.

SESAME BROCCOLI AND BELL PEPPER: Replace the greens beans with 1½ cups small broccoli florets, or 1 package (10 ounces) frozen broccoli florets.

MAKES 2 SERVINGS

Per serving:
98 calories
3 g protein
6 g fat (1 g sat)
8 g carbs
243 mg sodium
90 mg calcium
3 g fiber

SAVE FOR LATER

Stored in an airtight container, the extra serving of green beans and bell pepper will keep for 3 days in the refrigerator. Warm in a small saucepan over medium-low heat before serving.

Mashed Potatoes

MAKES 2 SERVINGS

Per serving:

181 calories

6 g protein

3 g fat (1 g sat)

29 g carbs

44 mg sodium

80 mg calcium

3 g fiber

Note: Analysis doesn't include sea salt and freshly ground black pepper to taste.

Although you can use any variety of potato to make mashed potatoes, many chefs and home cooks prefer to use Yukon golds because they have a naturally buttery taste. Use a potato masher or fork to mash them as smooth or chunky as you like, or beat them with an electric mixer for ultra-creamy mashed potatoes. Serve them plain or topped with Savory Onion Gravy (page 45).

> 2 large Yukon gold potatoes, peeled and cut into 2-inch cubes
> ¼ cup plain nondairy milk
> 1½ teaspoons vegan butter
> 1½ teaspoons nutritional yeast flakes
> Sea salt
> Freshly ground black pepper or white pepper

1. Put the potatoes in a large saucepan and cover with water. Cook over medium-high heat until soft, 20 to 25 minutes.

2. Drain the potatoes in a colander and return them to the saucepan.

3. Add the milk, butter, and nutritional yeast. Mash the potatoes with a potato masher or fork until they're as smooth as you like. Season with salt and pepper to taste. Serve hot.

CHEESY MASHED POTATOES: Add ¼ cup shredded vegan Cheddar cheese.

HERBED MASHED POTATOES: Add 1 tablespoon chopped fresh herbs (such as basil, chives, cilantro, dill, parsley, thyme, or rosemary), or 1 to 1½ teaspoons dried herbs.

SAVE FOR LATER

Stored in an airtight container, the extra serving of mashed potatoes will keep for 3 days in the refrigerator. Reheat the mashed potatoes in a small saucepan with 1 tablespoon of plain nondairy milk. Cook over medium heat, stirring constantly, until hot, 1 to 2 minutes. Alternatively, microwave the potatoes for 30 to 40 seconds.

Sweet Potato and Pecan Casserole

Cooked sweet potatoes are mashed with rich coconut milk and sweet maple syrup and then baked with a crunchy pecan topping. This delectable casserole is a popular side dish, especially for fall and winter holiday meals.

1 **pound** (3 medium) **sweet potatoes, peeled and cut into 2-inch cubes**

¼ cup plain or vanilla coconut milk beverage

1½ tablespoons maple syrup

2 teaspoons coconut oil

1 teaspoon ground cinnamon

½ teaspoon vanilla extract

⅓ cup coarsely chopped pecans

¼ teaspoon ground nutmeg

1. Put the sweet potatoes in a large saucepan and cover with water. Cook over medium-high heat until tender, 20 to 25 minutes.

2. Preheat the oven to 375 degrees F. Lightly oil an 8 x 4 x 2½-inch loaf pan or mist it with cooking spray.

3. Drain the sweet potatoes in a colander and return them to the saucepan.

4. Add the milk, 1 tablespoon of the maple syrup, 1½ teaspoons of the coconut oil, ½ teaspoon of the cinnamon, and the vanilla extract. Mash the sweet potatoes using a potato masher or fork until smooth and creamy. Transfer to the prepared loaf pan.

5. To make the topping, put the pecans and the remaining ½ teaspoon of maple syrup, remaining ½ teaspoon of coconut oil, remaining ½ teaspoon of cinnamon, and the nutmeg in a small bowl and stir until the pecans are evenly coated.

6. Distribute the seasoned pecans evenly over the sweet potatoes. Bake for 10 to 15 minutes, or until the pecans are lightly browned and fragrant. Serve hot.

BUTTERNUT SQUASH AND PECAN CASSEROLE: Replace the sweet potatoes with 1 small butternut squash (about 1 pound), peeled and cut into 2-inch cubes.

MAKES 2 SERVINGS

Per serving:

499 calories

5 g protein

19 g fat (5 g sat)

87 g carbs

175 mg sodium

210 mg calcium

9 g fiber

SAVE FOR LATER

Stored in an airtight container, the extra serving of sweet potato casserole will keep for 3 days in the refrigerator. To serve, preheat the oven to 350 degrees F. Transfer the sweet potatoes to a small ovenproof dish or pan and bake for about 15 minutes, or until hot. Alternatively, microwave the sweet potatoes for 30 to 40 seconds.

California Vegetables au Gratin

MAKES 2 SERVINGS

Per serving:

349 calories

7 g protein

6 g fat (0 g sat)

77 g carbs

127 mg sodium

115 mg calcium

7 g fiber

Frozen mixed California vegetables, a blend that includes sliced carrots along with broccoli and cauliflower florets, can be found in the freezer section of nearly all supermarkets. This pleasing combo is mixed with a vegan cheese sauce and sprinkled with a bread-crumb topping to create a colorful casserole.

1   slice whole-grain bread or other bread, torn into several pieces

2   tablespoons chopped fresh parsley

1½ teaspoons olive oil

1   package (10 ounces) frozen California mixed vegetables (broccoli, carrots, and cauliflower)

¾   cup Cashew Cheese Sauce (page 44) or Nutritional Yeast Cheese Sauce (page 43)

1. Preheat the oven to 375 degrees F. Lightly oil an 8 x 4 x 2½-inch loaf pan or mist it with cooking spray.

2. To make the topping, put the bread and parsley in a food processor and pulse or process into coarse bread crumbs. Add the oil and pulse several times to combine.

3. Put the vegetables and cheese sauce in the prepared loaf pan and stir to combine. Sprinkle the topping mixture evenly over the vegetables.

4. Bake for 15 to 18 minutes, or until the vegetables are tender and the topping is golden brown.

CREAMY CALIFORNIA VEGETABLES AU GRATIN: Replace the Cashew Cheese Sauce with ¾ cup Dairy-Free Béchamel Sauce (page 43).

VARIATION: Omit the bread, parsley, and oil and top the vegetable mixture with ½ cup crushed vegan buttery crackers or ½ cup French-fried onions.

SAVE FOR LATER

Stored in an airtight container, the extra serving of vegetables au gratin will keep for 3 days in the refrigerator. To serve, preheat the oven to 350 degrees F. Transfer the vegetables to a small ovenproof dish or pan and bake for about 15 minutes, or until hot. Alternatively, microwave the vegetables for 30 to 40 seconds.

Baked French Fries or Wedges

Skip the drive-thru and bake up a batch of French fries at home. Not only will they be a whole lot better for you, since they aren't deep-fried, but they also can be seasoned any way you like.

MAKES 2 SERVINGS

Per serving:

86 calories

3 g protein

5 g fat (1 g sat)

10 g carbs

220 mg sodium

0 mg calcium

1 g fiber

1   large russet potato or sweet potato, peeled

2   teaspoons nutritional yeast flakes

2   teaspoons olive oil or other oil

1   **teaspoon dried herbs** (such as basil, oregano, thyme, rosemary, or Italian seasoning)

1   teaspoon sweet paprika or chili powder

½   teaspoon garlic powder

¼   teaspoon sea salt

¼   teaspoon freshly ground black pepper

1. Preheat the oven to 425 degrees F. Line a baking sheet with parchment paper or a silicone baking mat.

2. Cut the potato into 3 x ½-inch-thick French fries or 8 wedges.

3. Put the potatoes, nutritional yeast, oil, herbs, paprika, garlic powder, salt, and pepper in a medium bowl and stir until the potatoes are evenly coated.

4. Transfer to the lined baking sheet and spread into a single layer. Bake for 20 minutes.

5. Remove from the oven, stir, then spread into a single layer again. Bake for 15 to 20 minutes longer, or until the potatoes are crisp and lightly browned around the edges. Serve hot.

ROOT VEGGIE TOTS: Replace the potato with 1½ to 2 cups of peeled and cubed beets, carrots, parsnips, or other root vegetables.

SPICED BAKED FRIES: Add your favorite spices, such as cayenne, cumin, or curry powder, along with or in place of the herbs and paprika.

SAVE FOR LATER

Stored in an airtight container, the extra serving of French fries or wedges will keep for 3 days in the refrigerator. To serve, preheat the oven to 350 degrees F and line a small baking sheet or pan with parchment paper. Transfer the fries or wedges to the lined baking sheet or pan and bake for about 10 minutes, or until hot.

Roasted Cauliflower

MAKES 2 SERVINGS

Per serving:

285 calories

16 g protein

12 g fat (2 g sat)

37 g carbs

215 mg sodium

230 mg calcium

16 g fiber

Steamed or boiled cauliflower can taste rather bland, but roasting it with seasonings and toasted sesame oil until the florets are golden brown imparts a sweet, nutty taste that's hard to resist. To heighten the flavor even more, squeeze a little lemon juice over the top.

1	head (1½ pounds) **cauliflower, cut into florets**
1½	**tablespoons nutritional yeast flakes**
1½	**tablespoons toasted sesame oil or olive oil**
¼	**teaspoon sea salt**
¼	**teaspoon freshly ground black pepper**
½	**lemon, cut into wedges** (optional)

1. Preheat the oven to 450 degrees F. Line a baking sheet with parchment paper or a silicone baking mat.

2. Put the cauliflower in a large bowl. Add the nutritional yeast, oil, salt, and pepper and stir until the florets are evenly coated.

3. Transfer to the lined baking sheet and spread into a single layer. Bake for 10 minutes.

4. Remove from the oven, stir, then spread into a single layer again. Bake for 10 to 15 minutes longer, or until the florets are crisp and lightly browned around the edges. Squeeze a little lemon juice over the florets if desired. Serve hot.

SPICED OR HERBED BAKED CAULIFLOWER: Season the cauliflower with ½ to 1 teaspoon of your favorite spices (such as curry powder, chili powder, paprika, or turmeric) or dried herbs (such as basil, oregano, or thyme) when you add the nutritional yeast.

SAVE FOR LATER

Stored in an airtight container, the extra serving of roasted cauliflower will keep for 3 days in the refrigerator. To serve, preheat the oven to 350 degrees F and line a small baking sheet or pan with parchment paper. Transfer the cauliflower to the lined baking sheet or pan and bake for about 10 minutes, or until hot.

Oven-Roasted Vegetables

You can easily amplify the flavor and natural sweetness of vegetables simply by roasting them in the oven. The how-to instructions in this recipe will guide you through the process. Use whatever vegetables you have on hand, and season them with your favorite oil, herbs, and spices.

4   **cups assorted vegetables** (such as bell peppers, broccoli, Brussels sprouts, cauliflower, eggplant, green beans, peeled winter squash, or peeled root vegetables), **cut into 1-inch cubes or ½-inch-thick slices**

1   **tablespoon olive oil or other oil**

1½ **tablespoons nutritional yeast flakes**

1   **tablespoon dried herbs** (such as basil, oregano, thyme, rosemary, or Italian seasoning)

¼   **teaspoon sea salt**

¼   **teaspoon freshly ground black pepper**

1. Preheat the oven to 450 degrees F. Line a baking sheet with parchment paper or a silicone baking mat.

2. Put the vegetables on the lined baking sheet. Drizzle the oil over the vegetables. Sprinkle evenly with the nutritional yeast, herbs, salt, and pepper. Using your hands, toss the vegetables until they are evenly coated, then spread into a single layer. Bake for 20 minutes.

3. Remove from the oven, stir, then spread into a single layer again. Bake for 10 to 15 minutes longer, or until the vegetables are tender and lightly browned around the edges. Serve hot.

MAKES 2 SERVINGS

Per serving:

195 calories

18 g protein

10 g fat (1 g sat)

86 g carbs

268 mg sodium

80 mg calcium

26 g fiber

SAVE FOR LATER

Stored in an airtight container, the extra serving of roasted vegetables will keep for 3 days in the refrigerator. To serve, preheat the oven to 350 degrees F and line a small baking sheet or pan with parchment paper. Transfer the vegetables to the lined baking sheet or pan and bake for about 10 minutes, or until hot.

Indian-Style Millet

MAKES 2 SERVINGS

Per serving:

81 calories

2 g protein

0 g fat (0 g sat)

18 g carbs

3 mg sodium

20 mg calcium

1 g fiber

Note: Analysis doesn't include sea salt and freshly ground black pepper to taste.

Turmeric is a ground spice that's often used in Indian cuisine. In fact, it's what gives curry powder its golden hue. In this dish, whole-grain millet is toasted and cooked with turmeric, dried fruit, and cilantro to create a quick accompaniment for vegetable curries or other Indian dishes.

½   cup millet, rinsed

1   cup water

1   teaspoon ground turmeric or curry powder

3   tablespoons chopped fresh cilantro

2   tablespoons dried currants, or ¼ cup raisins

Sea salt

Freshly ground black pepper

1. To toast the millet, put it in a medium saucepan and cook over medium heat, stirring occasionally, until the grains begin to "pop" and are lightly browned, 1 to 2 minutes.

2. Add the water and turmeric and stir to combine. Bring to a boil over high heat. Cover, decrease the heat to low, and simmer until the millet is tender and all the water is absorbed, 20 to 25 minutes.

3. Fluff the millet with a fork to separate the grains. Add the cilantro and currants and stir until evenly distributed. Season with salt and pepper to taste. Serve hot.

SAVE FOR LATER

Stored in an airtight container, the extra serving of millet will keep for 3 days in the refrigerator. Warm in a small saucepan over medium-low heat before serving.

Spanish Rice

Canned fire-roasted tomatoes give this Spanish rice a slightly smoky flavor, but if you can only find plain diced tomatoes in your area, it will still be delicious. Serve this spicy rice alongside tacos, burritos, or refried beans.

MAKES 2 SERVINGS

Per serving:

155 calories

3 g protein

6 g fat (1 g sat)

22 g carbs

24 mg sodium

30 mg calcium

3 g fiber

Note: Analysis doesn't include sea salt and freshly ground black pepper to taste.

¼ cup diced yellow onion	¼ cup water
¼ cup diced green bell pepper	½ teaspoon chili powder
½ jalapeño chile, seeded and finely diced	½ teaspoon dried oregano
2 teaspoons olive oil	¼ teaspoon ground cumin
½ cup long-grain brown or white rice, rinsed	¼ teaspoon sweet or smoked paprika
1½ teaspoons minced garlic	2 tablespoons chopped fresh cilantro
¾ cup diced fresh tomatoes or canned diced tomatoes (preferably fire-roasted with green chiles)	1 green onion, thinly sliced
	Sea salt
	Freshly ground black pepper

1. Put the onion, bell pepper, chile, and oil in a large nonstick skillet and cook over medium heat, stirring occasionally, for 3 minutes.

2. Add the rice and garlic and cook, stirring occasionally, for 1 minute.

3. Add the tomatoes, water, chili powder, oregano, cumin, and paprika and stir until well combined. Bring to a boil over high heat. Cover, decrease the heat to low, and simmer until the rice is tender and all the water is absorbed, 15 to 20 minutes for white rice or 30 to 40 minutes for brown rice.

4. Fluff the rice with a fork to separate the grains. Add the cilantro and green onion and stir until well incorporated. Season with salt and pepper to taste. Serve hot.

SPANISH QUINOA: Replace the rice with ½ cup quinoa, rinsed.

SPANISH RICE WITH CORN AND BEANS: Add ¼ cup canned or frozen corn kernels and ½ cup cooked or canned black, kidney, or pinto beans, drained and rinsed, after the rice is done cooking.

SAVE FOR LATER

Stored in an airtight container, the extra serving of rice will keep for 3 days in the refrigerator. Warm in a small saucepan over medium-low heat before serving.

Tricolor Quinoa with Collard Greens, Beans, and Pumpkin Seeds

MAKES 2 SERVINGS

Per serving:

327 calories

16 g protein

9 g fat (1 g sat)

53 g carbs

446 mg sodium

670 mg calcium

12 g fiber

Note: Analysis doesn't include sea salt and freshly ground black pepper to taste.

Tricolor quinoa is a blend of black, red, and white quinoa, but if you can't find it, any variety of quinoa can be used in this recipe. For added flavor, the quinoa is cooked in vegetable broth and then enhanced with collard greens, beans, parsley, and pumpkin seeds.

1¼	cups low-sodium vegetable broth
½	cup tricolor quinoa or other quinoa, rinsed
1	small shallot, diced, or ¼ cup diced red onion
2	teaspoons chopped fresh thyme, or ¾ teaspoon dried
1	large leaf collard greens or other leafy greens, stemmed and coarsely chopped
⅓	cup cooked or canned butter beans, kidney beans, or pinto beans, drained and rinsed
3	tablespoons raw or roasted pumpkin seeds
3	tablespoons chopped fresh parsley

Sea salt

Freshly ground black pepper

1. Put the broth, quinoa, shallot, and thyme in large saucepan and stir to combine. Bring to a boil over high heat. Cover, decrease the heat to low, and simmer until the quinoa is tender and all the broth is absorbed, 15 to 18 minutes.

2. Fluff the quinoa with a fork to separate the grains. Add the collard greens. Cover and let sit for 3 minutes to allow the collard greens to wilt.

4. Add the beans, pumpkin seeds, and parsley and stir until well incorporated. Season with salt and pepper to taste. Serve hot.

VARIATION: Replace the beans with 2 tablespoons dried fruit (such as cherries, cranberries, currants, or goji berries).

SAVE FOR LATER

Stored in an airtight container, the extra serving of quinoa will keep for 3 days in the refrigerator. Warm in a small saucepan over medium-low heat before serving.

Savory Stuffing

MAKES 2 SERVINGS

Per serving:

216 calories

7 g protein

7 g fat (1 g sat)

31 g carbs

885 mg sodium

250 mg calcium

3 g fiber

With just a few aromatic veggies and some vegetable broth, you can transform a stale loaf of bread into a savory side dish any time of the year or as part of a fall or winter holiday meal.

4	slices whole-grain bread or other bread, cut into 1-inch cubes
½	cup diced yellow onion
1	stalk celery, diced
1½	teaspoons olive oil
¼	cup thinly sliced green onion
¾	teaspoon dried thyme
½	teaspoon poultry seasoning
½	teaspoon sea salt
¼	teaspoon freshly ground black pepper
2	tablespoons chopped fresh parsley
1	tablespoon nutritional yeast flakes
¾	cup low-sodium vegetable broth

1. Put the bread cubes on a baking sheet and let air-dry for 1 hour.

2. Put the onion, celery, and oil in a large nonstick skillet and cook over medium heat, stirring occasionally, for 3 minutes.

3. Add the green onion, thyme, poultry seasoning, salt, and pepper and cook, stirring occasionally, for 1 minute. Remove from the heat.

4. Preheat the oven to 375 degrees F. Lightly oil an 8 x 4 x 2½-inch loaf pan or mist it with cooking spray.

5. Transfer the bread cubes to a large bowl. Add the onion mixture, parsley, and nutritional yeast and stir until well incorporated. Gently stir in the broth to moisten the bread cubes.

6. Transfer to the prepared loaf pan. Bake for 15 to 20 minutes, or until the stuffing is slightly dry and golden brown. Serve hot.

SAVE FOR LATER

Stored in an airtight container, the extra serving of stuffing will keep for 3 days in the refrigerator. To serve, preheat the oven to 350 degrees F and line a small baking sheet or pan with parchment paper. Transfer the stuffing to the lined baking sheet or pan and bake for about 10 minutes, or until hot.

NINE

Main Dishes

Easy Vegetable Fried Rice

MAKES 2 SERVINGS

Per serving:

277 calories

8 g protein

5 g fat (1 g sat)

55 g carbs

266 mg sodium

30 mg calcium

7 g fiber

Note: Analysis doesn't include freshly ground black pepper to taste.

Leftover cooked grain is great to have on hand, as it can easily be used in other recipes. If you've got some leftover rice in the fridge and a bag of mixed vegetables in the freezer, you can make this delicious dish in under ten minutes.

1	**package** (10 ounces) **frozen mixed vegetables** (carrots, corn, green beans, and peas)
½	**cup diced red bell pepper**
2	**teaspoons toasted sesame oil**
1	**cup cooked rice** (such as basmati, brown, or white rice)
2	**green onions, thinly sliced**
1	**tablespoon minced garlic**
1	**tablespoon peeled and grated fresh ginger**
2	**teaspoons reduced-sodium tamari**
	Freshly ground black pepper

1. Put the mixed vegetables, bell pepper, and oil in a large nonstick skillet and cook over medium heat, stirring occasionally, until almost tender, 5 to 7 minutes.

2. Add the rice, green onions, garlic, and ginger and cook, stirring occasionally, for 2 minutes.

3. Add the tamari and cook, stirring occasionally, until the vegetables are tender, 1 to 2 minutes. Season with pepper to taste. Serve hot.

EASY VEGETABLE FRIED MILLET OR QUINOA: Replace the cooked rice with 1 cup cooked millet or quinoa.

EASY VEGETABLE FRIED RICE WITH FRESH VEGGIES: Replace the frozen mixed vegetables with 1½ cups coarsely chopped assorted fresh vegetables (such as broccoli, cabbage, carrot, cauliflower, or onion).

PROTEIN-BOOSTED FRIED RICE: Add 1 cup diced firm tofu or canned beans, drained and rinsed, when adding the rice to the vegetables. Alternatively, sprinkle each serving with 2 tablespoons toasted chopped nuts or seeds.

SAVE FOR LATER

Stored in an airtight container, the extra serving of fried rice will keep for 3 days in the refrigerator. Warm in a small saucepan over medium-low heat before serving.

Veggie Stir-Fry

An assortment of colorful fresh vegetables are stir-fried until crisp-tender, then coated with a flavorful sauce that's flecked with bits of ginger and garlic. If you prefer, add or substitute other fresh or frozen vegetables to suit your taste. Serve the stir-fry over cooked rice, grains, or noodles.

MAKES 2 SERVINGS

Per serving:

122 calories

5 g protein

5 g fat (0 g sat)

26 g carbs

340 mg sodium

100 mg calcium

7 g fiber

Note: Analysis doesn't include sea salt and freshly ground black pepper to taste.

1	small Japanese eggplant, cut into 1-inch cubes
1	carrot, thinly sliced diagonally
½	cup red bell pepper, cut into 1-inch strips
½	cup thinly sliced shiitake or other mushrooms
1½	teaspoons sunflower oil or other oil
½	cup small broccoli or cauliflower florets
1	large stalk celery, thinly sliced diagonally
1	baby bok choy, cut into thin strips, or ¾ cup shredded green or red cabbage, lightly packed
¼	cup pea pods, cut in half diagonally, or 3 tablespoons frozen peas or edamame, thawed
3	tablespoons Stir-Fry Sauce or Sizzling Stir-Fry Sauce (page 42)

Sea salt

Freshly ground black pepper

1. Put the eggplant, carrot, bell pepper, mushrooms, and oil in a large nonstick skillet and cook over medium-high heat, stirring occasionally, for 5 minutes.

2. Add the broccoli and celery and cook, stirring occasionally, for 2 minutes.

3. Add the bok choy and pea pods and cook, stirring occasionally, until all the vegetables are crisp-tender, 2 to 3 minutes.

4. Add the stir-fry sauce and stir until evenly distributed. Season with salt and pepper to taste. Serve hot.

PROTEIN-BOOSTED VEGGIE STIR-FRY: Add ½ cup cubed tempeh, tofu, or seitan along with the eggplant.

SAVE FOR LATER

Stored in an airtight container, the extra serving of stir-fry will keep for 3 days in the refrigerator. Warm in a small saucepan over medium-low heat before serving.

Curried Lentils with Spinach

MAKES 2 SERVINGS

Per serving:

227 calories

16 g protein

3 g fat (0 g sat)

39 g carbs

74 mg sodium

150 mg calcium

20 g fiber

Note: Analysis doesn't include sea salt and freshly ground black pepper to taste.

Dried lentils are generously seasoned with curry powder and various spices and cooked with spinach until soft. Include the optional coconut milk if you want to add a bit of richness to the finished dish. Serve over cooked rice or grains.

1½ cups water

½ cup dried brown lentils, sorted and rinsed

⅓ cup diced yellow onion

1 stalk celery, diced

1½ teaspoons curry powder

1½ teaspoons minced garlic

½ teaspoon dried thyme

¼ teaspoon ground cumin

2 cups baby spinach, lightly packed, or 2 cups coarsely chopped spinach, lightly packed

3 tablespoons coconut milk (optional)

Sea salt

Freshly ground black pepper

1. Put the water, lentils, onion, celery, curry powder, garlic, thyme, and cumin in a large saucepan and stir to combine. Bring to a boil over high heat. Cover, decrease the heat to low, and simmer for 20 minutes.

2. Add the spinach and cook, stirring occasionally, until the lentils are tender and all the water is absorbed, 5 to 10 minutes.

3. Add the optional coconut milk and stir until well incorporated. Season with salt and pepper to taste.

BLACK-EYED PEAS WITH GREENS: Replace the lentils with ½ cup dried black-eyed peas, sorted and rinsed. Replace the spinach with 2 cups coarsely chopped turnip greens or collard greens.

MEDITERRANEAN LENTILS WITH SPINACH: Replace the curry powder and ground cumin with ¾ teaspoon dried basil and ½ teaspoon dried oregano or dried rosemary. Omit the coconut milk and add ⅓ cup diced tomato.

SAVE FOR LATER

Stored in an airtight container, the extra serving of curried lentils and spinach will keep for 3 days in the refrigerator. Warm in a small saucepan over medium-low heat before serving.

Tuscan Tempeh with Onion and Bell Pepper

To give tempeh a flavor boost, it's cubed and briefly marinated with a little balsamic vinegar and tamari. Next, the morsels are cooked with onion and bell pepper and then simmered in a tomato-based sauce. Serve this saucy mixture over cooked pasta or polenta or with crusty bread.

1   package (8 ounces) **tempeh, cut into ½-inch cubes**

1½ tablespoons balsamic vinegar

1   tablespoon reduced-sodium tamari

1   small red or yellow onion, cut into 1-inch strips

1   red or orange bell pepper, cut into 1-inch strips

2   teaspoons olive oil

1   tablespoon minced garlic

¾   cup canned crushed tomatoes, or ¾ cup marinara sauce

1   teaspoon Italian seasoning, or ½ teaspoon dried basil
    and ½ teaspoon dried oregano

¼   teaspoon crushed red pepper flakes (optional)

1½ teaspoons nutritional yeast flakes

    Sea salt

    Freshly ground black pepper

MAKES 3 SERVINGS

Per serving:

243 calories

18 g protein

12 g fat (2 g sat)

19 g carbs

462 mg sodium

89 mg calcium

2 g fiber

Note: Analysis doesn't include sea salt and freshly ground black pepper to taste.

1. Put the tempeh, vinegar, and tamari in a small bowl and stir to combine. Let sit for 5 minutes.

2. Put the onion, bell pepper, and oil in a large nonstick skillet and cook over medium heat, stirring occasionally, for 3 minutes.

3. Add the tempeh and garlic and cook, stirring occasionally, until the tempeh is lightly browned, 10 to 12 minutes.

4. Decrease the heat to low. Add the tomatoes, Italian seasoning, and optional red pepper flakes and cook, stirring occasionally, for 2 minutes.

5. Add the nutritional yeast and stir until well incorporated. Season with salt and pepper to taste. Serve hot.

TUSCAN TEMPEH WITH MUSHROOMS, ONION, AND BELL PEPPER: Add ½ cup thinly sliced button or crimini mushrooms when cooking the onion and bell pepper.

SAVE FOR LATER

Stored in an airtight container, the extra servings of tempeh with onion and bell pepper will keep for 3 days in the refrigerator. Warm in a small saucepan over medium-low heat before serving.

Deconstructed Veggie Lasagna

MAKES 2 SERVINGS

Per serving:

381 calories

16 g protein

11 g fat (2 g sat)

59 g carbs

168 mg sodium

130 mg calcium

5 g fiber

Note: Analysis doesn't include sea salt for boiling the pasta and freshly ground black pepper to taste.

At first glance this recipe may seem a bit complicated, but it's actually easy enough for even a novice cook to pull off. This enticing dish has all the flavors of a layered lasagna but with far less hassle. Both the vegetable and tofu ricotta mixtures can be made while the pasta is cooking.

Pinch sea salt (optional)

4   **ounces pasta** (such as penne, rotini, or ziti)

1   **cup frozen California mixed vegetables** (broccoli, carrots, and cauliflower) **or other frozen mixed vegetables**

¼   **cup diced red or yellow onion**

¼   **cup diced red bell pepper**

1½ **teaspoons olive oil**

2   **large cloves garlic, minced**

1   **teaspoon Italian seasoning, or ½ teaspoon dried basil and ½ teaspoon dried oregano**

4   **ounces firm or extra-firm tofu**

1   **tablespoon nutritional yeast flakes**

1   **tablespoon lemon juice**

¾   **cup marinara sauce**

¼   **cup shredded vegan mozzarella cheese**

Freshly ground black pepper

1. To cook the pasta, fill a large saucepan two-thirds full with water. Add the optional salt and bring to a boil over medium-high heat.

2. Add the pasta and cook, stirring occasionally, according to the package instructions or until tender. Reserve ¼ cup of the pasta water. Drain the pasta in a colander and return it to the saucepan.

3. While the pasta is cooking, make the vegetable mixture. Put the frozen vegetables, onion, bell pepper, and oil in a large nonstick skillet and cook over medium heat, stirring occasionally, for 5 minutes. Add the garlic and Italian seasoning and cook, stirring occasionally, until the vegetables are tender, 2 to 3 minutes.

SAVE FOR LATER

Stored in an airtight container, the extra serving of deconstructed lasagna will keep for 3 days in the refrigerator. Warm in a small saucepan or skillet over medium-low heat before serving.

4. While the vegetable mixture is cooking, make the tofu ricotta. Put the tofu, nutritional yeast, and lemon juice in a small bowl. Add the reserved pasta water and mash with a fork to combine.

5. Add the tofu mixture to the cooked pasta and stir until well incorporated.

6. Add the pasta mixture to the vegetable mixture in the skillet and stir to combine. Add the marinara sauce and cheese and stir until evenly distributed. Season with salt and pepper to taste. Serve hot.

DECONSTRUCTED WHITE VEGGIE LASAGNA: Replace the marinara sauce with ¾ cup Dairy-Free Béchamel Sauce (page 43).

Pesto Pasta with Spinach and Chickpeas

MAKES 2 SERVINGS

Per serving:

320 calories

14 g protein

8 g fat (1 g sat)

53 g carbs

270 mg sodium

90 mg calcium

5 g fiber

Note: Analysis doesn't include freshly ground black pepper and nutritional yeast flakes to taste.

Pesto adds a jolt of flavor to any dish. If you have pesto and baby spinach in the fridge and canned chickpeas in the pantry, you can be digging your fork into this pasta dish in under fifteen minutes.

Pinch sea salt (optional)

4 **ounces pasta** (such as penne, fettuccine, rotini, or spaghetti)

¼ **cup Pesto or Sun-Dried Tomato-Basil Pesto** (page 40)

2 **cups baby spinach, lightly packed**

⅓ **cup cooked or canned chickpeas or white beans** (such as cannellini or white kidney), **drained and rinsed**

Freshly ground black pepper

Nutritional yeast flakes

Crushed red pepper flakes (optional)

1. To cook the pasta, fill a large saucepan two-thirds full with water. Add the optional salt and bring to a boil over medium-high heat.

2. Add the pasta and cook, stirring occasionally, according to the package instructions or until tender. Reserve ¼ cup of the pasta water. Drain the pasta in a colander and return it to the saucepan.

3. Add the pesto and reserved pasta water and gently toss until the pasta is evenly coated.

4. Add the spinach and chickpeas and gently stir to combine. Season with pepper to taste. Garnish with nutritional yeast and red pepper flakes if desired. Serve hot.

PESTO PASTA WITH SPINACH AND ROASTED CHICKPEAS: Replace the cooked chickpeas with ⅓ cup Roasted Chickpea Croutons (page 54).

PESTO ZOODLES WITH SPINACH AND CHICKPEAS: Replace the cooked pasta with 1 medium zucchini that has been cut into noodle shapes with a spiralizer or vegetable peeler. Do not cook the zucchini noodles.

SAVE FOR LATER

Stored in an airtight container, the extra serving of pesto pasta will keep for 3 days in the refrigerator. Serve cold, or warm in a small saucepan over medium-low heat before serving.

Nutty Bulgur-Stuffed Peppers

Coarsely chopped walnuts are terrific for duplicating the taste and texture of ground meat in many recipes. In this one, they're sautéed with aromatic vegetables and seasonings before being combined with cooked bulgur to make the flavorful filling for these stuffed peppers.

2 large bell peppers

1 small yellow onion, finely diced

1 carrot, finely diced

1 tablespoon olive oil

½ cup coarsely chopped walnuts

3 large cloves garlic, minced

1 teaspoon Italian seasoning, or ½ teaspoon dried basil and ½ teaspoon dried oregano

1 cup cooked bulgur

¼ cup chopped fresh parsley, lightly packed

¼ cup water

1½ tablespoons tahini

1 tablespoon nutritional yeast flakes

Sea salt

Freshly ground black pepper

MAKES 2 SERVINGS

Per serving:

461 calories

12 g protein

34 g fat (4 g sat)

31 g carbs

33 mg sodium

90 mg calcium

13 g fiber

Note: Analysis doesn't include sea salt and freshly ground black pepper to taste.

1. Preheat the oven to 375 degrees F.

2. Cut the tops off the bell peppers, and remove and discard the ribs and seeds.

3. To make the filling, put the onion, carrot, and oil in a large nonstick skillet and cook over medium heat, stirring occasionally, for 3 minutes. Add the walnuts, garlic, and Italian seasoning and cook, stirring occasionally, until the walnuts are lightly browned and fragrant, 3 to 5 minutes.

4. Add the bulgur, parsley, water, tahini, and nutritional yeast and cook, stirring constantly, for 1 minute. Season with salt and pepper to taste.

5. Fill each pepper with half the filling mixture, then stand the peppers upright in an 8-inch baking pan. Bake for 20 to 25 minutes, or until the peppers are tender and the filling is hot.

SPANISH RICE STUFFED PEPPERS: Replace the filling with Spanish Rice or Spanish Rice with Corn and Beans (page 95).

VARIATION: Replace the bulgur with 1 cup cooked millet or quinoa.

SAVE FOR LATER

Stored in an airtight container, the extra stuffed pepper will keep for 3 days in the refrigerator. To serve warm, preheat the oven to 350 degrees F. Stand the pepper upright in a small baking dish and bake for 10 to 15 minutes, or until hot.

Swiss Chard and Sausage Stuffed Squash

Winter squash halves are stuffed with a sweet-and-savory mixture of Swiss chard, vegan sausage, dried cranberries, and crunchy sunflower seeds, then baked until soft. This is an excellent main dish to make during colder seasons or as part of a holiday meal.

1	**medium** (about 1 pound) **winter squash** (such as acorn, carnival, delicata, or small butternut)
2	vegan Italian sausages, coarsely chopped
1	shallot, diced, or ½ cup diced red or yellow onion
1	tablespoon olive oil
2	large leaves Swiss chard, leaves and stems thinly sliced
⅓	cup sunflower seeds, or ½ cup coarsely chopped nuts (such as almonds, pecans, or walnuts)
¼	cup dried cranberries
1	teaspoon Italian seasoning, or 1 teaspoon poultry seasoning
1½	tablespoons nutritional yeast flakes
	Sea salt
	Freshly ground black pepper

1. Preheat the oven to 375 degrees F.

2. Cut the winter squash in half (from the stem to the bottom). Using a spoon, scoop out and discard the seeds. Put the squash halves cut-side up in an 8-inch baking pan. Add a little water to the bottom of the baking pan. Bake for 15 minutes.

3. While the squash is baking, make the filling mixture. Put the vegan sausages, shallot, and oil in a large nonstick skillet and cook over medium heat, stirring occasionally, for 5 minutes.

4. Add the Swiss chard, sunflower seeds, cranberries, and Italian seasoning and cook, stirring occasionally, until the Swiss chard is wilted, 2 to 3 minutes. Add the nutritional yeast and stir until well incorporated. Season with salt and pepper to taste.

5. Remove the squash from the oven. Fill each squash half equally with the filling mixture. Bake for 10 to 15 minutes, or until the squash is tender. Serve hot.

SAVE FOR LATER

Stored in an airtight container, the extra serving of stuffed squash will keep for 3 days in the refrigerator. To serve, preheat the oven to 350 degrees F. Put the stuffed squash in a small baking dish and bake for 10 to 15 minutes, or until hot.

SWISS CHARD AND MUSHROOM STUFFED SQUASH: Replace the vegan sausages with 1½ cups coarsely chopped button or crimini mushrooms.

Breaded Tofu

**MAKES 4 PIECES,
2 SERVINGS**

Per serving:

230 calories

17 g protein

6 g fat (1 g sat)

29 g carbs

338 mg sodium

290 mg calcium

6 g fiber

Using a breading technique that's commonly used for chicken or fish, pieces of pressed tofu are dipped in a soy buttermilk mixture, then coated with seasoned bread crumbs. The breaded tofu can be either baked or fried until golden brown and served plain or topped with gravy.

8 ounces firm or extra-firm tofu, **pressed** (see tip, page 114)

¼ cup plain soy milk

¾ teaspoon lemon juice or cider vinegar

⅓ cup whole wheat flour or other flour

3 tablespoons dry bread crumbs or medium-grind cornmeal

2 tablespoons nutritional yeast flakes

1 teaspoon Italian seasoning, or ½ teaspoon dried basil and ½ teaspoon dried oregano

½ teaspoon garlic powder

½ teaspoon chili powder, or ¼ teaspoon smoked or sweet paprika

¼ teaspoon sea salt

⅛ teaspoon freshly ground black pepper

1. Preheat the oven to 400 degrees F. Line a baking sheet with parchment paper or a silicone baking mat.

2. Cut the tofu lengthwise into four slices.

3. To make the soy buttermilk, put the soy milk and lemon juice in a small bowl and stir to combine. Let sit for 5 minutes to thicken.

4. Put the flour on a large plate. Dip each tofu slice into the flour, evenly coating it on all sides. Put the coated slices on another large plate.

5. Add the bread crumbs, nutritional yeast, Italian seasoning, garlic powder, chili powder, salt, and pepper to the remaining flour on the plate and toss to combine using your fingers.

6. Working with one slice at a time, dip the tofu into the soy buttermilk and then into the bread crumb mixture, pressing down slightly and flipping the tofu over as needed to evenly coat all sides. Put the breaded slices on the lined baking sheet.

7. Bake for 15 minutes. Flip over the tofu slices. Bake for 10 to 15 minutes longer, or until the tofu is golden brown on both sides. Serve hot or cold.

SAVE FOR LATER

Stored in an airtight container, the extra serving of breaded tofu will keep for 3 days in the refrigerator. To serve warm, preheat the oven to 350 degrees F. Put the tofu in a small baking dish and bake for 10 to 15 minutes, or until hot.

BREADED TEMPEH: Replace the tofu with 1 package (8 ounces) tempeh. Cut the block of tempeh into four slices.

PAN-FRIED TOFU: For a crispier crust, the breaded tofu slices can be cooked in a little oil in a large nonstick skillet and over medium heat until golden brown, 5 to 7 minutes per side. Drain on paper towels to remove excess oil before serving.

Mac-n-Cheese

Macaroni and cheese is the ultimate comfort food. For ease, this vegan version is made with just cooked elbow macaroni and your choice of cheese sauce, which can be made quickly while the pasta is cooking.

Pinch sea salt (optional)

4   ounces elbow macaroni

1   cup Cashew Cheese Sauce (page 44) **or** Nutritional Yeast Cheese Sauce (page 43)

Freshly ground black pepper

MAKES 2 SERVINGS

Per serving:

448 calories

9 g protein

2 g fat (0 g sat)

90 g carbs

3 mg sodium

20 mg calcium

5 g fiber

Note: Analysis doesn't include freshly ground black pepper to taste.

1. To cook the pasta, fill a large saucepan two-thirds full with water. Add the optional salt and bring to a boil over medium-high heat.

2. Add the macaroni and cook, stirring occasionally, according to the package instructions or until tender. Drain the macaroni in a colander and return it to the saucepan.

3. Add the cheese sauce and stir until evenly distributed. Season with pepper to taste. Serve hot.

EXTRA CHEESY MAC-N-CHEESE: Add 1/3 cup shredded vegan Cheddar cheese along with the sauce.

FETTUCCINE WITH CASHEW ALFREDO: Replace the macaroni with 4 ounces fettuccine and use the Cashew Cheese Sauce. Pour the sauce over the cooked fettuccine and toss until evenly distributed.

VEGETABLE MAC-N-CHEESE: When the macaroni is almost done cooking, stir in 1/2 cup frozen broccoli florets or 1/4 cup frozen peas. Cook until both the macaroni and vegetables are tender.

SAVE FOR LATER

Stored in an airtight container, the extra serving of macaroni will keep for 3 days in the refrigerator. Warm in a small saucepan over medium-low heat before serving.

Barbecue Tofu or Tempeh

**MAKES 4 PIECES,
2 SERVINGS**

Per serving:

151 calories

10 g protein

5 g fat (1 g sat)

19 g carbs

441 mg sodium

240 mg calcium

2 g fiber

You only need two ingredients to make this super-simple yet delicious recipe: a package of tofu or tempeh and a bottle of your favorite barbecue sauce. Enjoy this as a main dish or cut it into cubes and add it to your favorite recipes.

> 8 ounces firm or extra-firm tofu, pressed (see tip), or 1 package (8 ounces) tempeh
>
> ⅓ cup barbecue sauce

1. Cut the tofu lengthwise into four pieces or cut the block of tempeh into four pieces.

2. Lightly oil an 8 x 4 x 2½-inch loaf pan or mist it with cooking spray. Spoon half the barbecue sauce into the loaf pan. Put the tofu or tempeh in the pan, then spoon the remaining sauce over it. Let marinate while the oven preheats.

3. Preheat the oven to 400 degrees F.

4. Bake for 15 minutes. Flip over the tofu or tempeh pieces. Bake for 15 minutes longer. Serve hot or cold.

TIP: Pressing tofu removes excess water, making it denser and meatier. To press it, gently squeeze the block of tofu over the sink to remove any excess water. Take care not to crush the tofu, as the block should remain intact. Put the tofu in a colander in the sink, then put a small plate directly on the tofu. Put a large can or other heavy weight on top of the plate and let the tofu rest and drain for 20 minutes.

BARBECUE TOFU OR TEMPEH SANDWICH: Layer two pieces of the hot or cold tofu or tempeh and ¼ cup Tangy Coleslaw or Classic Coleslaw (page 58) on a split bun or roll.

SAVE FOR LATER

Stored in an airtight container, the extra serving of barbecue tofu or tempeh will keep for 3 days in the refrigerator. To serve warm, preheat the oven to 350 degrees F. Put the tofu or tempeh in a small baking dish and bake for 10 to 15 minutes, or until hot.

Personal Pita Pizza

Craving pizza but frozen just won't do and your local shop doesn't offer vegan options? Well then, make your own using pita bread, which is the ideal size for a quick personal pizza. This classic combination can be enjoyed for a lunch, dinner, or snack.

1   (6-inch) **pita bread**

3   tablespoons **marinara sauce**

1½   tablespoons **sliced or diced red or yellow onion**

1½   tablespoons **sliced or diced red or orange bell pepper**

2   **button or crimini mushrooms, thinly sliced**

¼   cup **shredded vegan mozzarella cheese**

1   teaspoon **nutritional yeast flakes**

Freshly ground black pepper

Crushed red pepper flakes (optional)

1. Preheat the oven to 425 degrees F.

2. Put the pita bread on a baking sheet. Spread the marinara sauce evenly over the pita. Scatter the onion, bell pepper, and mushrooms over the sauce. Sprinkle the cheese and nutritional yeast over the vegetables, then sprinkle with pepper and red pepper flakes if desired.

3. Bake for 8 to 10 minutes, or until the pita bread is lightly browned around the edges and the cheese is melted. Cut into 4 pieces. Serve hot.

MEATY PERSONAL PIZZA: Add crumbled vegan sausage or pepperoni slices before baking.

MEDITERRANEAN PITA PIZZA: Replace the marinara sauce with 3 tablespoons Hummus (page 34). Replace the bell pepper with ½ cup baby spinach, lightly packed, and replace the mushrooms with 1 tablespoon sliced kalamata olives.

PITA PIZZA WITH PESTO, TOMATOES, AND ARTICHOKES: Replace the marinara sauce with 2 tablespoons Pesto (page 40). Replace the onion, bell pepper, and mushrooms with 4 cherry tomatoes, halved, and 2 canned or jarred artichoke hearts, quartered.

MAKES 1 SERVING

Per serving:

292 calories

9 g protein

8 g fat (2 g sat)

47 g carbs

568 mg sodium

10 mg calcium

7 g fiber

Note: Analysis doesn't include freshly ground black pepper to taste.

Cookies, Bars, and Sweet Treats

CHAPTER
TEN

Chocolate Chip Cookies

For many people, chocolate chip cookies reign supreme in the world of desserts. Although you can find vegan chocolate chips in virtually any grocery store, if you have vegan chocolate bars in the house, you can replace the chips with an equal amount of coarsely chopped chocolate.

1½ tablespoons warm water

½ teaspoon chia seeds, or 1 teaspoon ground flaxseeds or flaxseed meal

¼ cup coconut oil, melted

¼ cup unbleached cane sugar

¼ cup light brown sugar, lightly packed

1 teaspoon vanilla extract

1 cup whole wheat pastry flour

½ teaspoon baking soda

¼ teaspoon baking powder

¼ teaspoon sea salt

½ cup vegan chocolate chips or carob chips

1. Preheat the oven to 350 degrees F. Line a baking sheet with parchment paper or a silicone baking mat.

2. Put the water and chia seeds in a medium bowl and stir to combine. Let rest for 10 minutes, until the mixture thickens into a gel.

3. Add the oil, cane sugar, brown sugar, and vanilla extract and stir to combine. Add the flour, baking soda, baking powder, and salt and stir to combine. Gently stir in the chocolate chips.

4. Portion the dough onto the lined baking sheet using 1 heaping tablespoon for each cookie. Space the cookies two inches apart. Slightly flatten each one with wet fingers.

5. Bake for 10 to 12 minutes, or until lightly browned on the bottom and around the edges. Let cool completely on the baking sheet.

GLUTEN-FREE CHOCOLATE CHIP COOKIES: Replace the whole wheat pastry flour with 1 cup gluten-free baking mix and add ¼ teaspoon xanthan or guar gum (if the baking mix doesn't contain any).

LOADED CHOCOLATE CHIP COOKIES: Add ¼ cup unsweetened shredded dried coconut and/or coarsely chopped pecans or walnuts.

MAKES 12 COOKIES

Per cookie:

139 calories

2 g protein

8 g fat (6 g sat)

22 g carbs

91 mg sodium

0 mg calcium

2 g fiber

SAVE FOR LATER

Stored in an airtight container, the extra cookies will keep for 5 days at room temperature or 2 months in the freezer.

Oatmeal Raisin Cookies

MAKES 12 COOKIES

Per cookie:

96 calories

2 g protein

3 g fat (1 g sat)

15 g carbs

143 mg sodium

0 mg calcium

1 g fiber

Old-fashioned rolled oats do double duty in these chewy cookies, as some of the oats are processed into a flour while the remainder are left intact in the dough. The cookies are flavored with an alluring combination of maple syrup, cinnamon, ginger, raisins, and sunflower seeds.

1¾ cups old-fashioned rolled oats

1 teaspoon baking soda

½ teaspoon ground cinnamon

¼ teaspoon ground ginger

¼ teaspoon sea salt

¼ cup sunflower oil or coconut oil, melted

¼ cup maple syrup

1 teaspoon vanilla extract

⅓ cup raisins

¼ cup sunflower seeds or coarsely chopped walnuts

1. Preheat the oven to 375 degrees F. Line a baking sheet with parchment paper or a silicone baking mat.

2. Put 1 cup plus 2 tablespoons of the rolled oats in a food processor and process into a powdery flour. Transfer the oat flour to a medium bowl.

3. Add the remaining ⅔ cup of rolled oats and the baking soda, cinnamon, ginger, and salt and stir to combine. Add the oil, maple syrup, and vanilla extract and stir to combine. Gently stir in the raisins and sunflower seeds.

4. Portion the dough onto the lined baking sheet using 1 heaping tablespoon for each cookie. Space the cookies two inches apart. Slightly flatten each one with wet fingers.

5. Bake for 10 to 12 minutes, or until lightly browned on the bottom and around the edges. Let cool completely on the baking sheet.

VARIATION: Replace the raisins with ⅓ cup whole or coarsely chopped dried fruit, such as apricots, cherries, cranberries, currants, dates, or figs, or a combination.

SAVE FOR LATER

Stored in an airtight container, the extra cookies will keep for 5 days at room temperature or 2 months in the freezer.

Nut Butter Cookies

Just because you're allergic to peanuts doesn't mean you still can't enjoy a nut butter cookie. In fact, any kind of nut butter can be used to make these scrumptious treats, which have a sugary coating and the classic crisscross pattern on top.

MAKES 12 COOKIES

Per cookie:

85 calories

2 g protein

4 g fat (1 g sat)

11 g carbs

72 mg sodium

10 mg calcium

2 g fiber

1½ tablespoons warm water

1 teaspoon ground flaxseeds or flaxseed meal (preferably golden flaxseeds)

2½ tablespoons unbleached cane sugar

3 tablespoons nut butter (such as almond, cashew, or peanut)

2 tablespoons vegan butter

1½ tablespoons light brown sugar, lightly packed

¼ teaspoon vanilla extract

½ cup whole wheat pastry flour

¼ teaspoon baking soda

⅛ teaspoon sea salt

1. Preheat the oven to 375 degrees F. Line a baking sheet with parchment paper or a silicone baking mat.

2. Put the water and flaxseeds in a medium bowl and stir to combine. Let rest for 10 minutes, until the mixture thickens into a gel.

3. Put 1 tablespoon of the cane sugar in a small bowl and set aside.

4. Add the remaining 1½ tablespoons of cane sugar to the flaxseed mixture along with the nut butter, butter, brown sugar, and vanilla extract and stir to combine. Add the flour, baking soda, and salt and stir to combine.

5. Roll the dough into one-inch balls, then roll each ball in the reserved cane sugar until evenly coated. Arrange the balls on the lined baking sheet, spacing them two inches apart. Flatten each ball slightly with a fork to create a crisscross pattern with the tines.

6. Bake for 8 to 10 minutes, or until lightly browned on the bottom and around the edges. Let cool completely on the baking sheet.

SAVE FOR LATER

Stored in an airtight container, the extra cookies will keep for 5 days at room temperature or 2 months in the freezer.

Rich and Chewy Brownies

MAKES 6 BROWNIES

Per brownie:

264 calories

4 g protein

11 g fat (4 g sat)

40 g carbs

126 mg sodium

0 mg calcium

3 g fiber

Coffee, chocolate chips, and cacao powder unite to create the deep dark-chocolate flavor of these chewy, rich-tasting brownies. If you like, add the optional chopped nuts to the batter or sprinkle them over the top of the batter to add a little crunch.

1½ tablespoons warm water

½ teaspoon chia seeds, or 1½ teaspoons ground flaxseeds or flaxseed meal (preferably golden flaxseeds)

6 tablespoons vegan chocolate chips

2 tablespoons brewed coffee (regular or decaffeinated) or water

1½ tablespoons vegan butter

½ cup unbleached cane sugar

¼ cup cacao powder or unsweetened cocoa powder

½ teaspoon vanilla extract

¾ cup unbleached all-purpose flour or whole wheat pastry flour

¼ teaspoon sea salt

⅛ teaspoon baking soda

¼ cup coarsely chopped walnuts or pecans (optional)

1. Preheat the oven to 350 degrees F. Line an 8 x 4 x 2½-inch loaf pan with two pieces of parchment paper, overlapping the pieces and allowing the paper to drape a bit over the sides of the pan.

2. Put the water and chia seeds in a small bowl and stir to combine. Let rest for 10 minutes, until the mixture thickens into a gel.

3. Put the chocolate chips, coffee, and butter in a small glass or ceramic bowl and microwave in intervals of 10 to 15 seconds, stirring between each interval, until the chips are melted. Alternatively, put the chocolate chips, coffee, and butter in a double boiler over medium-low heat until the chips are melted. Transfer to a large bowl.

4. Add the sugar, cacao powder, and vanilla extract and stir until the sugar dissolves. Add the flour, salt, and baking soda and stir to form a thick batter. Gently stir in the optional chopped walnuts (or sprinkle them over the batter, as described in the next step).

SAVE FOR LATER

Stored in an airtight container, the extra brownies will keep for 5 days at room temperature or 2 months in the freezer.

5. Transfer to the lined loaf pan and press the batter evenly into the pan using a silicone spatula. If the optional walnuts weren't added to the batter, you can sprinkle them over the top of the batter now. Bake for 20 to 22 minutes, or until the top feels dry. Let cool for 15 minutes in the pan, then lift out of the pan using the parchment paper and transfer to a rack to cool completely. Cut into 6 pieces with a sharp knife.

Raw Energy Balls

MAKES 12 BALLS

Per ball:

116 calories

3 g protein

6 g fat (1 g sat)

14 g carbs

1 mg sodium

20 mg calcium

2 g fiber

With the help of a food processor, you can quickly pulverize raw nuts, seeds, and dried fruit to make these guilt-free treats. Satisfy your craving for something sweet and increase your energy level naturally by nibbling one or more of these energy balls.

⅓   **cup nuts** (such as almonds, Brazil nuts, cashews, pecans, pistachios, or walnuts)

¼   **cup sunflower seeds or pumpkin seeds**

1½ **tablespoons hemp seeds, or 1½ teaspoons chia seeds**

½   **cup pitted soft dates** (preferably medjool), **lightly packed**

¼   **cup raisins**

¼   **cup dried cranberries, cherries, or goji berries, or a combination**

¼   **cup unsweetened shredded dried coconut**

1   **teaspoon maca powder** (optional)

1   **teaspoon peeled and grated fresh ginger, or ¼ teaspoon ground ginger**

1. Put the nuts, sunflower seeds, and hemp seeds in a food processor and process until finely ground.

2. Add the dates, raisins, cranberries, coconut, optional maca powder, and ginger and process until the mixture comes together to form a ball, 1 to 2 minutes.

3. Dampen your hands with water and form the mixture into twelve 1-inch balls.

SAVE FOR LATER

Stored in an airtight container, the energy balls will keep for 1 week in the refrigerator or 3 months in the freezer.

Caramel-Almond Blondies

You'll be pleasantly surprised by the caramel undertone in these blondies, which is created by a combination of brown sugar, agave nectar, optional maca powder, and almond and vanilla extracts. In addition, almond butter is used instead of oil or butter to give these blondies a moist, tender crumb.

MAKES 6 BLONDIES

Per blondie:

196 calories

5 g protein

10 g fat (1 g sat)

23 g carbs

103 mg sodium

60 mg calcium

2 g fiber

3   tablespoons warm water

½   teaspoon chia seeds, or 1½ teaspoons ground flaxseeds or flaxseed meal (preferably golden flaxseeds)

6   tablespoons almond butter

¼   cup light brown sugar, lightly packed

1   tablespoon agave nectar

½   teaspoon almond extract

½   teaspoon vanilla extract

½   cup unbleached all-purpose flour

1½   teaspoons maca powder (optional)

⅛   teaspoon baking soda

⅛   teaspoon sea salt

3   tablespoons sliced almonds, or ¼ cup coarsely chopped almonds

1. Preheat the oven to 350 degrees F. Line an 8 x 4 x 2½-inch loaf pan with two pieces of parchment paper, overlapping the pieces and allowing the paper to drape a bit over the sides of the pan.

2. Put 1½ tablespoons of the water and the chia seeds in a large bowl and stir to combine. Let rest for 10 minutes, until the mixture thickens into a gel.

3. Add the remaining 1½ tablespoons of water and the almond butter, brown sugar, agave nectar, almond extract, and vanilla extract and stir to combine. Add the flour, optional maca powder, baking soda, and salt and stir to form a thick batter. Gently stir in the almonds.

4. Transfer to the lined loaf pan and press the batter evenly into the pan using your hands. Bake for 20 to 22 minutes, or until the top feels dry. Let cool in the pan for 15 minutes, then lift out of the pan using the parchment paper and transfer to a rack to cool completely. Cut into 6 pieces with a sharp knife.

SAVE FOR LATER

Stored in an airtight container, the extra blondies will keep for 5 days at room temperature or 2 months in the freezer.

No-Bake Dried-Fruit Cereal Bars

MAKES 6 BARS

Per bar:

219 calories

7 g protein

10 g fat (2 g sat)

29 g carbs

58 mg sodium

40 mg calcium

4 g fiber

Sweet and crunchy is the perfect way to describe these fruity, fiber-rich bars. They're made with a blend of rolled oats, crispy rice cereal, shredded coconut, crunchy seeds, and dried fruit. Enjoy them as snack or an on-the-go breakfast.

½ **cup old-fashioned rolled oats**

2 **tablespoons unsweetened shredded dried coconut**

2 **tablespoons pumpkin seeds**

1 **tablespoon sunflower seeds**

1 **cup crispy or puffed rice cereal**

¼ **cup whole or coarsely chopped dried fruit** (such as apricots, cherries, cranberries, currants, dates, figs, or goji berries, or a combination)

1 **tablespoon flaxseeds or hemp seeds** (optional)

¼ **cup nut butter** (any kind)

¼ **cup brown rice syrup or maple syrup**

½ **teaspoon vanilla extract**

Pinch sea salt

1. Line an 8 x 4 x 2½-inch loaf pan with two pieces of parchment paper, overlapping the pieces and allowing the paper to drape a bit over the sides of the pan.

2. Put the oats, coconut, pumpkin seeds, and sunflower seeds in a large nonstick skillet and cook over medium heat, stirring occasionally, until the mixture is fragrant, about 3 minutes. Transfer to a large bowl.

3. Add the cereal, dried fruit, and optional flaxseeds and gently stir to combine.

4. Put the nut butter and brown rice syrup in the skillet and cook over low heat, stirring occasionally, until thoroughly heated and small bubbles begin to appear around the edges, 1 to 2 minutes. Remove from the heat. Add the vanilla extract and salt and stir to combine.

5. Pour the nut butter mixture over the oat mixture and gently stir until well incorporated.

SAVE FOR LATER

Stored in an airtight container, the cereal bars will keep for 1 week in the refrigerator.

6. Transfer to the lined loaf pan. Fold the overhanging parchment paper over the top, and use it to press the mixture firmly and evenly into the pan. Refrigerate until firm, about 30 minutes.

7. Lift out of the pan using the parchment paper, transfer to a cutting board, and remove and discard the parchment paper. Cut into 6 bars with a sharp knife.

Buckeyes

MAKES 10 BUCKEYES

Per buckeye:

113 calories

2 g protein

7 g fat (3 g sat)

13 g carbs

30 mg sodium

0 mg calcium

1 g fiber

The great state of Ohio is famous for its buckeyes, the ones that fall from the trees as well as the chocolate-covered peanut butter candies that resemble them. Only four ingredients are needed to create these highly addictive confections.

⅔ cup powdered sugar

¼ cup creamy peanut butter

1   tablespoon coconut oil, melted

⅓ cup vegan chocolate chips

1. Line a large plate with parchment or waxed paper.

2. Put the sugar, peanut butter, and oil in a small bowl and mix with your hands to form a soft dough.

3. Form the mixture into ten 1-inch balls and put them on the lined plate as they are made. Refrigerate until firm, about 1 hour.

4. Put the chocolate chips in a small glass or ceramic bowl and microwave in intervals of 10 to 15 seconds, stirring between each interval, until the chips are melted. Alternatively, put the chocolate chips in a double boiler over medium-low heat until melted.

5. To coat each buckeye, put one peanut butter ball in the melted chocolate. Use a fork to roll the ball around until three-quarters of the surface is covered. Leave a small circle of the peanut butter filling visible on top. Use the fork to remove the coated ball from the chocolate and return it to the lined plate. Repeat the process with the remaining balls and chocolate. Refrigerate for 30 minutes before serving.

PEANUT BUTTER TRUFFLES: Increase the chocolate chips to ½ cup. Proceed as directed for the main recipe but fully cover each peanut butter ball with the melted chocolate.

SAVE FOR LATER

Stored in an airtight container, the buckeyes will keep for 2 weeks in the refrigerator.

Strawberry-Banana Soft-Serve Ice Cream

With the use of a food processor, you can transform a frozen banana and some strawberries into a lusciously creamy, soft-serve ice cream. Enjoy it right away as is, or top it with additional chopped fruit or nuts.

MAKES 1 SERVING

Per serving:
129 calories
2 g protein
1 g fat (0 g sat)
33 g carbs
7 mg sodium
47 mg calcium
4 g fiber

1   very ripe banana, frozen

⅔   cup sliced strawberries, or 4 whole frozen strawberries
     (do not thaw)

1½ teaspoons plain or vanilla nondairy milk or water

1. Break the banana into three pieces.
2. Put the banana, strawberries, and milk in a food processor and process until smooth, 1 to 2 minutes. Serve immediately.

CHOCOLATE, PEANUT BUTTER, AND BANANA SOFT-SERVE ICE CREAM: Replace the strawberries with 2 tablespoons peanut butter and 1½ tablespoons cacao powder or unsweetened cocoa powder.

MAPLE-PECAN SOFT-SERVE ICE CREAM: Use 1 large very ripe banana and omit the strawberries. Replace the nondairy milk with 1½ teaspoons maple syrup. Stir 2 tablespoons coarsely chopped toasted pecans into the finished ice cream.

SOFT-SERVE ICE-CREAM SUNDAE: Top the ice cream with chopped fresh or dried fruit and nuts and drizzle with Dark Chocolate Sauce (page 39).

Silken Berry Pudding

MAKES 3 SERVINGS

Per serving:

158 calories

9 g protein

3 g fat (0 g sat)

26 g carbs

70 mg sodium

130 mg calcium

2 g fiber

Soft-textured silken tofu is ideal for creating creamy desserts like this velvety pudding, which is made by blending silken tofu with juicy berries, a little lemon juice, and your choice of sweetener. Serve the chilled pudding plain or topped with additional fresh berries or diced or sliced fruit.

2   **cups fresh berries** (such as blackberries, blueberries, raspberries, or strawberries, or a combination), **or 1 pound frozen berries, thawed**

1   **package** (12 ounces) **silken firm or extra-firm tofu**

3   **tablespoons unbleached cane sugar, agave nectar, or maple syrup**

1. Put all the ingredients in a food processor or blender and process for 1 minute. Scrape down the work bowl or blender jar and process until completely smooth.

2. Transfer to a medium bowl. Cover and refrigerate for at least 30 minutes before serving. Serve cold or at room temperature.

SILKEN CHERRY PUDDING: Replace the berries with 2 cups pitted fresh or frozen cherries, thawed. Sweeten to taste with 1 to 2 tablespoons of additional sugar.

SILKEN PEACH PUDDING: Replace the berries with 2 cups peeled and sliced fresh peaches or frozen sliced peaches, thawed.

SAVE FOR LATER

Stored in an airtight container, the extra pudding will keep for 3 days in the refrigerator.

Tropical Chia Pudding Parfait

Chia seeds magically thicken coconut milk into a creamy pudding. The chilled chia pudding is then layered with diced mango and kiwi, shredded coconut, and sliced almonds to create a surprisingly healthy parfait.

MAKES 1 SERVING

Per serving:

492 calories

13 g protein

22 g fat (5 g sat)

68 g carbs

106 mg sodium

66 mg calcium

16 g fiber

⅔ cup plain or vanilla coconut milk beverage or other nondairy milk

1½ tablespoons chia seeds

2 teaspoons agave nectar

¼ teaspoon vanilla extract

½ mango, peeled and diced

1 kiwi, peeled and diced

1 tablespoon unsweetened shredded dried coconut

1 tablespoon sliced almonds

1. To make the chia pudding, put the milk, chia seeds, agave nectar, and vanilla extract in a small bowl and whisk to combine. Let rest for 10 minutes to thicken. Whisk the chia mixture again to break up any clumps of chia seeds.

2. Refrigerate until the mixture thickens into a pudding, about 20 minutes.

3. To assemble the parfait, put half of the chia pudding in a tall glass or bowl. Top with half of the mango and kiwi and half of the shredded coconut. Repeat the layers once more. Scatter the almonds over the top. Serve immediately.

VARIATION: Replace the mango and kiwi with other whole or diced fresh fruit or berries.

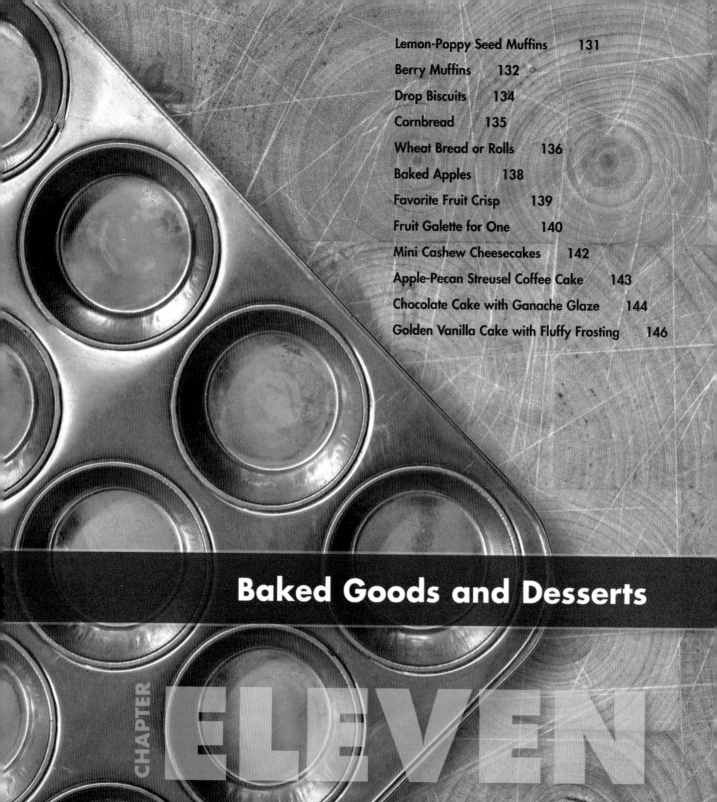

Baked Goods and Desserts

CHAPTER ELEVEN

Lemon-Poppy Seed Muffins

Brighten your day with these eye-appealing muffins, which are made with fresh lemon zest and juice and crunchy poppy seeds. Using safflower oil and a pinch of turmeric gives them a sunny yellow tint.

MAKES 6 MUFFINS

Per muffin:

186 calories

2 g protein

7 g fat (1 g sat)

27 g carbs

159 mg sodium

40 mg calcium

1 g fiber

1   cup unbleached all-purpose flour

1   teaspoon baking powder

½   teaspoon baking soda

⅛   teaspoon sea salt

Pinch turmeric

¼   cup plain nondairy milk

¼   cup agave nectar

3   tablespoons safflower oil or other oil

Zest and juice of ½ lemon (¾ teaspoon zest and 2 tablespoons juice)

1   tablespoon poppy seeds

1   teaspoon vanilla extract

1. Preheat the oven to 400 degrees F. Line six cups of a standard muffin tin with paper or silicone liners, or lightly oil or mist the cups with cooking spray.

2. Put the flour, baking powder, baking soda, salt, and turmeric in a medium bowl and whisk to combine.

3. Add the milk, agave nectar, oil, lemon zest and juice, poppy seeds, and vanilla extract and whisk to combine.

4. Fill the prepared muffin cups three-quarters full. Bake for 18 to 20 minutes, or until a toothpick inserted in the center of a muffin comes out clean.

5. Let cool in the pan for 5 minutes, then transfer the muffins to a rack. Serve warm or at room temperature.

LIME-COCONUT MUFFINS: Replace the lemon zest and juice with the zest and juice of 1 lime (2 teaspoons zest and 2 tablespoons juice). Replace the poppy seeds with ¼ cup unsweetened shredded dried coconut.

ORANGE-POPPY SEED MUFFINS: Replace the lemon zest and juice with 1 teaspoon orange zest and 2 tablespoons orange juice.

SAVE FOR LATER

Stored in an airtight container, the extra muffins will keep for 3 days at room temperature or 2 months in the freezer.

Berry Muffins

MAKES 6 MUFFINS

Per muffin:

161 calories

2 g protein

6 g fat (1 g sat)

24 g carbs

148 mg sodium

70 mg calcium

1 g fiber

These quick and easy muffins are bursting with berries. They can be enjoyed for breakfast or as an afternoon snack with a cup of tea or coffee.

1   **cup plus 2 tablespoons unbleached all-purpose flour or whole wheat pastry flour**

2   **tablespoons unbleached cane sugar**

2¼ **teaspoons baking powder**

¼ **teaspoon sea salt**

⅔ **cup plain nondairy milk**

2½ **tablespoons sunflower oil or other oil**

½ **teaspoon vanilla extract**

½ **cup fresh or frozen berries** (such as blueberries, blackberries, cranberries, or raspberries)

1. Preheat the oven to 400 degrees F. Line six cups of a standard muffin tin with paper or silicone liners, or lightly oil or mist the cups with cooking spray.

2. Put the flour, sugar, baking powder, and salt in a medium bowl and whisk to combine.

3. Add the milk, oil, and vanilla extract and whisk to combine. Gently stir in the berries.

4. Fill the prepared muffin cups three-quarters full. Bake for 18 to 20 minutes, or until a toothpick inserted in the center of a muffin comes out clean.

5. Let cool in the pan for 5 minutes, then transfer the muffins to a rack. Serve warm or at room temperature.

VARIATION: Replace the berries with ½ cup chopped fresh fruit, ¼ cup dried fruit, ½ cup coarsely chopped nuts, or ½ cup vegan chocolate chips, or any combination of these.

SAVE FOR LATER

Stored in an airtight container, the extra muffins will keep for 3 days at room temperature or 2 months in the freezer.

Drop Biscuits

MAKES 4 BISCUITS

Per biscuit:
220 calories
6 g protein
10 g fat (2 g sat)
28 g carbs
292 mg sodium
0 mg calcium
4 g fiber

In the time that it takes to preheat the oven, you not only can prepare the biscuit dough but also can have the biscuits portioned on the baking sheet. These drop biscuits are unbelievably quick and easy, and they taste so yummy when topped with vegan butter or jam.

⅓ cup plain nondairy milk

1 teaspoon cider vinegar

1¼ cups whole wheat pastry flour

1 tablespoon nutritional yeast flakes

2½ teaspoons baking powder

¼ teaspoon sea salt

2½ tablespoons safflower oil or other oil

1. Preheat the oven to 400 degrees F. Line a baking sheet with parchment paper or a silicone baking mat.

2. Put the milk and vinegar in a small bowl and stir to combine. Let rest for 5 minutes to thicken.

3. Put the flour, nutritional yeast, baking powder, and salt in a medium bowl and stir to combine.

4. Add the milk mixture and oil and stir to combine.

5. Portion the biscuits using a ¼-cup measuring cup and drop them onto the lined baking sheet, spacing them two inches apart.

6. Bake for 10 to 12 minutes, or until lightly browned on the bottom and around the edges. Serve hot, warm, or at room temperature.

CHEESY DROP BISCUITS: Add ⅓ cup shredded vegan cheese along with the milk mixture in step 4. Store the baked biscuits in an airtight container in the refrigerator.

HERBED DROP BISCUITS: Add 2 teaspoons dried herbs (such as basil, dill, thyme, parsley, or rosemary, or a combination) or 2 to 3 tablespoons chopped fresh herbs along with the milk mixture in step 4.

SAVE FOR LATER

Stored in an airtight container, the extra biscuits will keep for 3 days at room temperature or 2 months in the freezer.

Cornbread

Cornbread is a classic recipe that's beloved by nearly everyone. It's the perfect accompaniment to a bowl of chili, stew, or soup. Leftovers make a terrific breakfast topped with vegan butter and jam, or a savory snack topped with salsa.

¾ cup fine or medium-grind cornmeal

½ cup whole wheat pastry flour or spelt flour

2 teaspoons baking powder

1½ teaspoons unbleached cane sugar

¼ teaspoon sea salt

⅔ cup plain nondairy milk

2 tablespoons safflower oil or other oil

1. Preheat the oven to 400 degrees F. Lightly oil an 8 x 4 x 2½-inch loaf pan or mist it with cooking spray.

2. Put the cornmeal, flour, baking powder, sugar, and salt in a medium bowl and whisk to combine.

3. Add the milk and oil and whisk to combine.

4. Pour into the prepared pan and smooth the top with a silicone spatula.

5. Bake for 18 to 20 minutes, or until a toothpick inserted in the center of the cornbread comes out clean. Serve warm or at room temperature.

CHEDDAR-JALAPEÑO CORNBREAD: Add 3 tablespoons shredded vegan Cheddar cheese and 1 jalapeño chile, seeded and finely diced, along with the milk and oil in step 3.

GLUTEN-FREE CORNBREAD: Replace the whole wheat pastry flour with 6 tablespoons almond flour and 2 tablespoons tapioca starch.

MAKES 6 PIECES

Per piece:

187 calories

3 g protein

5 g fat (1 g sat)

33 g carbs

133 mg sodium

60 mg calcium

3 g fiber

SAVE FOR LATER

Stored in an airtight container, the extra cornbread will keep for 3 days at room temperature or 2 months in the freezer.

Wheat Bread or Rolls

MAKES 1 LOAF (8 SLICES), 2 SMALL LOAVES (4 SLICES EACH), OR 8 ROLLS

Per slice or roll:

199 calories

7 g protein

5 g fat (1 g sat)

36 g carbs

221 mg sodium

20 mg calcium

5 g fiber

Making homemade bread or rolls is really quite simple and fun. Using a combination of flours produces an easy-to-work-with dough that can be used for either a loaf or rolls. The result is bread with a soft texture and a slightly nutty flavor.

1   **cup warm water** (between 110 and 115 degrees F)

1½   **cups whole wheat flour**

2   **tablespoons unbleached cane sugar**

1   **package** (.25 ounce) **or 2¼ teaspoons active dry yeast**

1½   **cups unbleached all-purpose flour or white whole wheat flour**

2   **tablespoons nutritional yeast flakes**

2   **tablespoons olive oil or other oil, plus additional for drizzling**

1   **teaspoon sea salt**

1. Put the water, ½ cup of the whole wheat flour, and the sugar and yeast in a large bowl and stir to combine. Let rest until small bubbles appear on the surface, about 10 minutes.

2. Add the remaining cup of whole wheat flour, 1¼ cups of the all-purpose flour, and the nutritional yeast, oil, and salt. Stir to form a slightly shaggy dough.

3. Transfer to a clean work surface. Using your hands, knead for 3 to 5 minutes, working in the remaining ¼ cup of all-purpose flour as needed to prevent sticking and to make a soft, smooth dough.

4. Drizzle a little oil around the outer edge and bottom of the same large bowl. Roll the dough around in it, turning it over to coat it with oil on all sides. Cover the bowl with plastic wrap or a clean towel. Let rise in a warm place until double in size, about 1½ hours.

5. Punch down the dough. Transfer the dough to a clean work surface and knead for 1 minute.

6. To make a large loaf of bread, roll the dough into an eight-inch log. Lightly oil an 8 x 4 x 2½-inch loaf pan or mist it with cooking spray. Put the shaped loaf into the prepared pan and cover with plastic wrap or a clean towel. Let rise for 30 minutes.

Alternatively, to make two small loaves, divide the dough in half. Shape each half into a four-inch log or circle. Freeze one small loaf for later use (see sidebar). Line a baking sheet with parchment paper or with a silicone baking mat, and put the remaining small loaf on the lined baking sheet. Cover with plastic wrap or a clean towel and let rise for 30 minutes.

To make rolls, roll the dough into an eight-inch log, then cut it into eight pieces. Roll each piece into a ball. Line a baking sheet with parchment paper or a silicone baking mat, and arrange the balls on the lined baking sheet, spacing them two inches apart. Cover with plastic wrap or a clean towel and let rise for 30 minutes.

7. While the dough is rising, preheat the oven to 375 degrees F.

8. Bake a large loaf for 30 minutes, a small loaf for 20 to 22 minutes, or rolls for 12 to 15 minutes, until lightly browned. Let cool slightly, then transfer to a rack to finish cooling. Serve warm or at room temperature.

SAVE FOR LATER

Stored in an airtight container, the extra baked bread or rolls will keep for 3 days at room temperature. Alternatively, to bake later, the shaped small loaf or rolls can be frozen until solid on the lined baking sheet. Transfer to an airtight container and store in the freezer for up to 1 month. Thaw the small bread or desired number of rolls in the refrigerator for 8 to 12 hours. Transfer to a lined baking sheet. Cover, let rise for 30 minutes, preheat the oven per step 7 of the recipe, then bake as directed in step 8.

Baked Apples

MAKES 2 SERVINGS

Per serving:

300 calories

2 g protein

10 g fat (1 g sat)

57 g carbs

2 mg sodium

90 mg calcium

8 g fiber

Simple and scrumptious! Cored apples are filled with a spiced nut and dried-fruit filling and then baked until tender. Use very firm apples, as that will ensure they'll hold their shape while they bake. Serve the apples plain or topped with maple syrup and vegan yogurt.

2   **large apples** (such as Braeburn, Cortland, Fuji, Gala, or Granny Smith)

2   **tablespoons coarsely chopped pecans or walnuts**

2   **tablespoons raisins or dried cranberries**

2   **pitted soft dates** (preferably medjool), **coarsely chopped, or 2 dried figs, coarsely chopped**

1   **tablespoon maple syrup**

¼   **teaspoon ground cinnamon**

1. Preheat the oven to 375 degrees F.

2. Using a knife or vegetable peeler, remove the core from each apple (do not go all the way through the apple) and discard it. Remove a one-inch strip of peel from the top of each apple.

3. To make the filling, put the pecans, raisins, dates, maple syrup, and cinnamon in a small bowl and stir to combine. Fill each apple cavity with half of the filling mixture.

4. Put the apples in an 8 x 4 x 2½-inch loaf pan. Fill the pan with one-half inch of water. Cover and bake for 30 to 35 minutes, or until the apples are tender. Let cool for 5 minutes before serving.

SAVE FOR LATER

Stored in an airtight container, the extra baked apple will keep for 2 days in the refrigerator.

Favorite Fruit Crisp

Fruit crisp is an old-fashioned dessert that never gets old. Use your favorite fruit or a combination of fruit, as any kind will taste great once it's been sugared and spiced and baked with a crumbly topping. Serve it plain or topped with a scoop of non-dairy ice cream.

4   cups fresh or frozen sliced fruit or berries (such as apples, blueberries, peaches, pears, plums, raspberries, rhubarb, or strawberries, or a combination)

1½ teaspoons lemon juice

½   cup light brown sugar, lightly packed

1   teaspoon ground cinnamon

½   teaspoon ground ginger or cardamom

1   cup old-fashioned rolled oats

⅓   cup whole wheat pastry flour, barley flour, or almond flour

¼   cup vegan butter

½   teaspoon vanilla extract

1. Preheat the oven to 375 degrees F. Lightly oil an 8-inch square baking pan or mist it with cooking spray.

2. Put the fruit and lemon juice in the baking pan and stir to combine.

3. Put the brown sugar, cinnamon, and ginger in a medium bowl and stir to combine. Sprinkle half the sugar mixture over the fruit and stir until well incorporated.

4. Add the oats and flour to the remaining sugar mixture and stir to combine. Add the butter and vanilla extract and use a fork to work them into the oat mixture to form coarse crumbs. Sprinkle the oat mixture over the fruit.

5. Bake for 30 to 35 minutes, or until the topping is golden brown and the filling is bubbly. Let cool 5 minutes before serving.

MAKES 3 SERVINGS

Per serving:

481 calories

7 g protein

18 g fat (4 g sat)

78 g carbs

136 mg sodium

199 mg calcium

9 g fiber

SAVE FOR LATER

Stored in an airtight container, the extra servings of fruit crisp will keep for 3 days in the refrigerator.

Fruit Galette for One

MAKES 1 SERVING

Per serving:

413 calories

7 g protein

18 g fat (5 g sat)

60 g carbs

372 mg sodium

40 mg calcium

7 g fiber

A galette is a rustic pie that isn't assembled in a pie pan. Instead, the pie crust is rolled into a circle on parchment paper, the fruit filling is placed in the center, and then the filling is partially covered by folding and pleating the crust around the edges. Use your favorite fruit to fill this single-serving galette.

GALETTE CRUST

7 tablespoons whole wheat pastry flour, or ½ cup almond flour

1 teaspoon unbleached cane sugar

⅛ teaspoon sea salt

2½ tablespoons vegan butter

1 tablespoon cold water

½ teaspoon cider vinegar

FILLING

½ cup diced fruit or fresh or frozen berries (such as apple, blueberries, peach, pear, plum, nectarine, raspberries, or strawberries, or a combination)

1½ teaspoons unbleached cane sugar, plus additional for sprinkling

1 teaspoon cornstarch or arrowroot

⅛ teaspoon ground cinnamon or cardamom (optional)

1. To make the crust, put the flour, sugar, and salt in a small bowl and stir to combine. Add the butter, water, and vinegar and work them into the flour mixture using a fork to make a soft dough. Put in the freezer for 10 minutes.

2. Preheat the oven to 375 degrees F.

3. Put the crust mixture between two 9-inch pieces of parchment paper or two silicone baking mats. Roll it into a seven-inch circle using a rolling pin. Transfer to a baking sheet by lifting the crust with the bottom piece of parchment paper. Remove and discard the top sheet of parchment paper.

4. To make the filling, put the fruit, sugar, cornstarch, and optional cinnamon in a small bowl and stir to combine. Mound the filling into the center of the crust circle.

5. Lightly dampen the outer edge of the crust with water. Fold up the edges of the crust to create a one-inch border around the filling, pleating and pressing down on the crust as needed to maintain the circular shape. Lightly dampen the crust's border with water, and sprinkle a little sugar over it.

6. Bake for 25 to 30 minutes, or until the crust is lightly browned. Let cool for 5 minutes. Serve warm or at room temperature.

Mini Cashew Cheesecakes

MAKES 6 MINI CHEESECAKES

Per mini cheesecake:

222 calories

6 g protein

18 g fat (6 g sat)

17 g carbs

4 mg sodium

220 mg calcium

2 g fiber

Rather than being baked like standard cheesecakes, these raw mini versions are chilled in the freezer to firm up both the nutty date crust and the cashew-based filling. Serve them plain or garnished with Dark Chocolate Sauce (page 39) or chopped fruit or berries.

CRUST

⅔ cup raw nuts
(such as almonds, pecans, or walnuts)

⅓ cup pitted soft dates
(preferably medjool), lightly packed

FILLING

1 cup raw cashews, soaked in water for 2 hours and drained

2 tablespoons agave nectar

2 tablespoons coconut oil, melted

2 teaspoons lemon juice

1 teaspoon vanilla extract

1. Line six cups of a standard muffin tin with paper or silicone liners, or lightly oil or mist the cups with cooking spray.

2. To make the crust, put the nuts in a food processor and process until finely ground. Add the dates and process until the mixture comes together to form a ball, about 1 minute. Put 2 heaping tablespoons of the crust mixture into each muffin cup, and firmly flatten with your fingers to cover the bottom of each cup. Put in the freezer until slightly firm, about 10 minutes.

3. To make the filling, put all the ingredients in the food processor and process until smooth and creamy, 2 to 3 minutes, stopping once to scrape down the work bowl. Evenly divide the filling mixture among the muffin cups. Cover with waxed paper or a clean towel and put in the freezer until firm, at least 4 hours.

4. Loosen the sides of the mini cheesecakes from the pan with a table knife and remove them from the muffin tin 10 minutes prior to serving.

CASHEW CHEESECAKE BARS: Prepare the recipe using an 8 x 4 x 2½-inch loaf pan. Line the pan with two pieces of parchment paper, overlapping the pieces and allowing the paper to drape a bit over the sides of the pan. Cut the finished cheesecake into six pieces with a sharp knife.

MINI CHOCOLATE CASHEW CHEESECAKES: When processing the filling, add 3 tablespoons cacao powder or unsweetened cocoa powder.

SAVE FOR LATER

Stored in an airtight container, the extra mini cheesecakes will keep for 1 week in the refrigerator or 3 months the freezer.

Apple-Pecan Streusel Coffee Cake

Chopped pecans are added to the sweet streusel mixture that tops this moist coffee cake, which is enhanced with both chopped apple and applesauce.

MAKES 6 PIECES

Per piece:

269 calories

4 g protein

8 g fat (1 g sat)

48 g carbs

70 mg sodium

40 mg calcium

7 g fiber

STREUSEL TOPPING

- ¼ cup whole wheat pastry flour
- ¼ cup light brown sugar, lightly packed
- 2 tablespoons unbleached cane sugar
- ¼ teaspoon ground cinnamon
- ⅛ teaspoon ground nutmeg
- 2 tablespoons vegan butter
- 2 tablespoons finely chopped pecans

CAKE

- ¾ cup whole wheat pastry flour
- ¼ cup unbleached cane sugar
- 1½ teaspoons baking powder
- ½ teaspoon ground cinnamon
- ⅛ teaspoon sea salt
- ½ cup plain nondairy milk
- ¼ cup applesauce
- 1 teaspoon vanilla extract
- 1 small apple, peeled, cored, and finely chopped

1. Preheat the oven to 400 degrees F. Lightly oil an 8 x 4 x 2½-inch loaf pan or mist it with cooking spray.

2. To make the streusel topping, put the flour, brown sugar, cane sugar, cinnamon, and nutmeg in a small bowl. Add the butter and use a fork to work it into the flour mixture to form coarse crumbs. Stir in the pecans.

3. To make the cake, put the flour, sugar, baking powder, cinnamon, and salt in a medium bowl and whisk to combine. Add the milk, applesauce, and vanilla extract and whisk to combine. Gently stir in the apple.

4. Transfer the batter to the prepared pan and smooth the top with a silicone spatula. Sprinkle the streusel topping evenly over the batter.

5. Bake for 20 to 25 minutes, or until a toothpick inserted in the center of the cake comes out clean. Serve warm or at room temperature.

SAVE FOR LATER

Stored in an airtight container, the extra coffee cake will keep for 3 days at room temperature.

Chocolate Cake with Ganache Glaze

To intensify the rich, chocolaty flavor of this cake, both cacao powder and chocolate nondairy milk are used. But if you only have plain nondairy milk on hand, feel free to use that instead; the cake will still taste delicious, especially since it's covered with a luxurious chocolate ganache glaze.

CAKE

½ cup whole wheat pastry flour

3   tablespoons cacao powder or unsweetened cocoa powder

¼   teaspoon plus ⅛ teaspoon baking powder

¼   teaspoon baking soda

¼   teaspoon sea salt

⅓   cup maple syrup or agave nectar

3   tablespoons chocolate or plain nondairy milk

2   tablespoons sunflower oil or other oil

½   teaspoon vanilla extract

½   teaspoon cider vinegar

CHOCOLATE GANACHE

½   cup vegan chocolate chips

2½ tablespoons plain nondairy milk

1. Preheat the oven to 350 degrees F. Lightly oil an 8 x 4 x 2½-inch loaf pan or mist it with cooking spray.

2. To make the cake, put the flour, cacao powder, baking powder, baking soda, and salt in a large bowl and whisk to combine.

3. Add the maple syrup, milk, oil, vanilla extract, and vinegar and whisk to combine. Transfer the batter to the prepared pan and smooth the top with a silicone spatula.

4. Bake for 20 to 25 minutes, or until a toothpick inserted in the center of the cake comes out clean. Let cool in the pan for 5 minutes. Loosen the sides of the cake from the pan with a table knife. Invert the pan onto a rack and let the cake release naturally from the pan.

Put the rack on top of a baking sheet. Let the cake cool completely before glazing.

5. To make the chocolate ganache, put the chocolate chips and milk in a medium glass or ceramic bowl and microwave in intervals of 10 to 15 seconds, stirring between each interval, until the chips are melted. Alternatively, put the chocolate chips in a double boiler over medium-low heat until melted.

6. To glaze the cake, leave the cooled cake on the rack. Slowly pour half the chocolate ganache over the top of the cake, and use a silicone spatula or table knife to help spread the ganache over the sides of the cake. Let sit for 10 minutes. Repeat the procedure with the remaining ganache. Refrigerate the cake for 15 minutes before serving to allow the ganache to harden.

FANCY CHOCOLATE CAKE WITH GANACHE GLAZE: After the second coating of ganache, let the cake sit at room temperature for 10 minutes. Sprinkle the top with cacao nibs, shredded coconut, or chopped nuts, then refrigerate for 5 minutes. Alternatively, decorate the top of the finished cake with whole or sliced berries.

SAVE FOR LATER

Stored in an airtight container, the cake will keep for 3 days in the refrigerator.

Golden Vanilla Cake with Fluffy Frosting

A combination of vegan buttermilk, coconut oil, and vanilla extract work together to add a bit of tanginess and complexity to the flavor of this golden cake, which is covered with a light and fluffy frosting. If you like, decorate the top of the cake with sliced fruit or berries or a dusting of vegan sprinkles, shredded coconut, or chopped nuts.

CAKE

½ cup plain or vanilla soy milk or almond milk

1 teaspoon cider vinegar

6 tablespoons unbleached cane sugar

3 tablespoons coconut oil, melted

1½ teaspoons vanilla extract

¾ cup unbleached all-purpose flour

¾ teaspoon baking powder

¼ teaspoon baking soda

¼ teaspoon sea salt

FROSTING

½ cup powdered sugar

1 tablespoon vegan butter

1½ teaspoons plain or vanilla soy milk or almond milk

⅛ teaspoon vanilla extract

1. Preheat the oven to 350 degrees F. Lightly oil an 8 x 4 x 2½-inch loaf pan or mist it with cooking spray.

2. To make the cake, put the milk and vinegar in a large bowl and stir to combine. Let rest for 5 minutes to thicken.

3. Add the sugar, oil, and vanilla extract and whisk until the sugar is dissolved.

4. Put the flour, baking powder, baking soda, and salt in a medium bowl and stir to combine. Add the flour mixture to the milk mixture and whisk to combine. Transfer the batter to the prepared pan and smooth the top with a silicone spatula.

SAVE FOR LATER

Stored in an airtight container, the extra cake will keep for 3 days in the refrigerator.

5. Bake for 20 to 25 minutes, or until a toothpick inserted in the center of the cake comes out clean. Let cool in the pan for 5 minutes. Loosen the sides of the cake from the pan with a table knife. Invert the pan onto a rack and let the cake release naturally from the pan. Let cool completely before frosting.

6. To make the frosting, put all the ingredients in a large bowl and beat with an electric mixer on medium speed until light and fluffy, 2 to 3 minutes. Alternatively, put all the ingredients in a food processor and process until light and fluffy, 1 to 2 minutes. Spread the frosting over the top of the cake using a silicone spatula or table knife.

TIP: To make a single-layer round cake, double the ingredients for the cake batter and frosting and bake in an 8-inch round cake pan.

INDEX

BookPublishing Co.

books that educate, inspire, and empower

Visit **BookPubCo.com** to find your favorite books on plant-based cooking and nutrition, raw foods, and healthy living.

BOOKS BY ELLEN JAFFE JONES

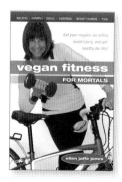

Paleo Vegan
with recipes by Alan Roettinger
978-1-57067-305-4 • $16.95

Vegan Fitness for Mortals
978-1-57067-340-5 • $14.95

Eat Vegan on $4 a Day
978-1-57067-257-6 • $14.95

BOOKS BY BEVERLY LYNN BENNETT

Chia
978-1-55312-049-0 • $11.95

Anti-Inflammatory Foods and Recipes
978-1-57067-341-2 • $17.95

Spiralize!
978-1-55312-052-0 • $11.95

Purchase these titles from your favorite book source or buy them directly from:
Book Publishing Company • PO Box 99 • Summertown, TN 38483 • 1-888-260-8458

Free shipping and handling on all orders